mustsees
Pacific Northwest
Featuring National Parks

Sunset, San Juan Islands, Washington ©Michael Bertrand

mustsees **Pacific Northwest**

Editorial Director	Cynthia Clayton Ochterbeck
Editorial Manager	Gwen Cannon
Contributing Writer	Leslie Forsberg
Production Manager	Natasha G. George
Cartography	Peter Wrenn
Photo Researcher	Nicole D. Jordan
Layout	Nicole D. Jordan
Additional Layout	Natasha G. George
Cover & Interior Design	Chris Bell, cbdesign
Cover Design & Layout	Natasha G. George

Contact Us	Michelin Travel and Lifestyle North America
	One Parkway South
	Greenville, SC 29615, USA
	travel.lifestyle@us.michelin.com
	www.michelintravel.com
	Michelin Travel Partner
	Hannay House
	39 Clarendon Road
	Watford, Herts WD17 1JA, UK
	www.ViaMichelin.com
	travelpubsales@uk.michelin.com
Special Sales	For information regarding bulk sales, customized
	editions and premium sales, please contact us at:
	travel.lifestyle@us.michelin.com
	www.michelintravel.com

Michelin Travel Partner

Société par actions simplifiées au capital de 11 288 880 EUR
27 cours de l'Île Seguin - 92100 Boulogne Billancourt (France)
R.C.S. Nanterre 433 677 721

© 2013 Michelin Travel Partner
ISBN 978-2-067182-04-2
Printing: PRINTER TRENTO, Trento (Italy)
Printed and bound in Italy: October 2013

Note to the reader:
While every effort is made to ensure that all information printed in this guide is correct
and up-to-date, Michelin Travel Partner accepts no liability for any direct, indirect or
consequential losses howsoever caused so far as such can be excluded by law. Admission
prices listed for sights in this guide are for a single adult, unless otherwise specified.

Welcome to Pacific Northwest

p.75

©Washington State Parks and Recreation

p.107

©The Oregon Garden

TABLE OF CONTENTS

©Torsten Kjellstrand / www.travelportland.com

p.102

TABLE OF CONTENTS

★★★ ATTRACTIONS

Unmissable historic, cultural and natural sights

©National Park Service

Fort Vancouver National
Historic Site p 83

©MountStHelens.com

Mount St. Helens p 79

©Russ Veenema

Pacific Coast Beaches p 40

MUST KNOW

Woodland Park Zoo p 54

©Ryan Hawk/Woodland Park Zoo

Oregon Dunes National Recreation Area p 113

©U.S. Department of Agriculture

PUBLIC MARKET

Pike Place Market p 52

©Tim Thompson/Seattle's Convention and Visitors Bureau

★★★ ATTRACTIONS

Unmissable historic, cultural and natural sights

For more than 75 years people have used Michelin stars to take the guesswork out of travel. Our star-rating system helps you make the best decision as to where to go, what to do and what to see.

★★★	Unmissable
★★	Worth a trip
★	Worth a detour
No star	Recommended

★★★Three Star

Crater Lake NP *p 36*
Fort Vancouver NHS *p 83*
Johnston Ridge Observatory *p 81*
Mount Rainier NP *p 37*
Mount St. Helens NVM *p 79*
Lan Su Chinese Garden *p 97*
Olympic NP *p 39*
Oregon Dunes NRA *p 113*
Pacific Coast Beaches *p 40*
Pacific Rim NPR *p 42*
Paradise *p 38*
Pike Place Market *p 52*
Royal BC Museum *p 132*
Seattle *p 44*
Seattle Art Museum *p 50*
Stanley Park *p 131*
UBC Museum of Anthropology *p 132*
Vancouver *p 128*
Victoria *p 128*
Woodland Park Zoo *p 54*

★★Two Star

Astoria *p 110*
Cape Perpetua Scenic Area *p 113*
Chittenden Locks *p 52*
Columbia Gorge *p 99*
Ecola State Park *p 114*
EMP Museum *p 50*
Evergreen Aviation & Space Museum *p 106*
Fort Clatsop *p 112*
Fort Nisqually Living History Museum *p 70*
Green Lake *p 55*
Hart and Steens *p 123*
Hells Canyon Scenic Byway *p 123*
High Desert Museum *p 119*
Klondike Gold Rush NHP *p 53*
Long Beach Peninsula *p 81*
Lopez Island *p 66*

Makah Cultural and Research Center *p 78*
MOHAI *p 50*
Mount Hood *p 100*
Museum at Warm Springs *p 119*
Museum of Glass *p 70*
Newberry NVM *p 121*
North Cascades NP *p 39*
Northwest Trek Wildlife Park *p 84*
Orcas Island *p 66*
Oregon Coast Aquarium *p 115*
Oregon Garden *p 107*
Oregon History Center *p 96*
Oregon Museum of Science and Industry *p 98*
Oregon Zoo *p 98*
Pacific Science Center *p 54*
Portland *p 92*
Portland Art Museum *p 96*
Port Townsend *p 73*
San Juan Islands *p 65*
Sea Lion Caves *p 115*
Seattle Center *p 46*
Seattle Asian Art Museum *p 54*
Snoqualmie Falls *p 60*
Tacoma Art Museum *p 70*
Tamástslikt Cultural Institute *p 119*
Trail of Ten Falls *p 107*
Washington Park *p 97*
Washington State History Museum *p 70*
Yaquina Head ONA *p 113*

★One Star

A.C. Gilbert's Discovery Village *p 108*
Alki Beach *p 55*
Bainbridge Island *p 60*
Baker City *p 118*
Bellevue *p 61*
Bellingham *p 68*
Bend *p 117*
Burke Museum *p 51*

ACTIVITIES

Unmissable activities, entertainment, restaurants and hotels

The Pacific Northwest's splendid topography and vibrant communities hold plenty of diversions for visitors. We recommend every activity in this guide, but the Michelin Man logo highlights our top picks.

Outings
Go apple-picking *p 86*
Stay at a lodge *p 147*
Stroll in a garden *p 131*
Look for whales *p 111*
Visit a museum *p 98*

Hotels
Cave B Inn & Spa *p 149*
The Nines *p 150*
Inn at the Market *p 145*
Woodmark Hotel *p 146*
Fairmont Empress
  p 156

Nightlife
Century Ballroom *p 59*
Crystal Ballroom *p 102*
Dimitriou's Jazz Alley
  p 59
Jimmy Mak's *p 102*
Triple Door *p 59*

Relax
Beachcomb *p 114*
Fly a kite *p 82*
Peer at boats *p 52*
Sip some wine *p 103*
Take afternoon tea
  p 130

Restaurants
C Restaurant *p 143*
Clarklewis *p 139*
Flying Fish *p 135*
The Walrus & The
  Carpenter *p 136*
Willows Inn *p 137*

Shopping
The Bellevue
  Collection *p 61*
Nob Hill *p 101*
Pearl District *p 102*
Pacific Place *p 58*
University Village *p 58*

Sports
Golfing *p 115*
Hiking *p 41, 68, 103*
Kayaking *p 65*
Skiing *p 100*
River rafting *p 127*

Side Trips
Columbia Gorge *p 99*
Mount Hood *p 100*
San Juan Islands *p 65*
Whidbey Island *p 66*

Drives
Columbia River
  Highway *p 99*
Crater Rim Drive *p 36*
Hells Canyon *p 123*
Hood Canal *p 78*
Hood River County
  Fruit Loop *p 99*

IDEAS AND TOURS

Throughout this thematic guide you will find inspiration for many different ways to experience the Pacific Northwest. The following is a selection of places and activities from the guide to help start you off. The sights in bold are found in the index.

SEASIDE SERENITY

Ocean swells travel miles across the open Pacific before reaching the sand beaches or rocky ramparts of the Pacific Northwest's vast coastlines. Oregon and Washington combined boast more than 450mi of ocean shores, including the 172-island **San Juan Islands**★★ archipelago in the great inland sea of Puget Sound. Wildlife abounds throughout, with whales, sea lions and countless shorebirds common sights.

Washington's coastlines are remarkably diverse. The wind-whipped, driftwood-tumbled wilderness beaches of **Olympic Peninsula**★★★ are the region's most remote shorelines; these pristine natural areas offer dramatic seascapes. **Second Beach** and **Third Beach** have miles of soft sand and tree-topped sea stacks. Even more remarkable are the dense, moss-cloaked rain forest valleys—**Hoh Rain Forest**★★★ and **Quinault Rain Forest**★★, just inland, backing the beaches. Here, protected by **Olympic National Park**★★★, old-growth trees tower over a landscape rich with biodiversity.

Oregon's beaches are easily accessed, and contain some of the region's most spectacular settings. East of Portland, **Ecola State Park**★★ has expansive views of sea stacks marching south along the coastline. On the Central Coast, Newport is home to the **Oregon Coast Aquarium**★★. Farther south, **Cape Perpetua Scenic Area**★★ features tide pools and wave-driven spouts, on a rugged headland. Rare Steller sea lions congregate at **Sea Lion Caves**★★. **Oregon Dunes National Recreation Area**★★★ myriad recreational options, from sandboarding to dune-buggy riding.

San Juan Islands

©Mark Gardner/San Juan Islands Visitors Bureau

MUST KNOW

MAJESTIC MOUNTAINS

Pacific Northwest is home to two massive mountain ranges: the **Cascade Range**, which divides Washington and Oregon into the wetter western side and the dryer east side, and the **Olympic Range**, on the **Olympic Peninsula** west of Seattle. Both provide a spider's web of trails alongside streams to mountain lakes or up switchbacks to sky-high vantage points. One of the most-accessible peaks to drive to is **Hurricane Ridge★★★**, in Port Angeles, surrounded by jagged-toothed mountains. Wildlife ranges from deer and (more rarely) bears to raccoons and marmots. Famed among hardcore skiers and snowboarders, **Mount Baker**, soaring 10,788ft in the North Cascades, provides as much as 65ft of snow every winter; summer here means hiking, and blueberry-filled meadows in the fall.

Farther east, the **North Cascades National Park★★** is accessible mainly to hikers and backpackers who trek into glacial cirques or mountain passes from trailheads off the **North Cascades Scenic Highway★★**.

South of Seattle, ice-bound **Mount Rainier★★★** soars skyward 14,410ft. Numerous trails here offer entrance to wildflower-filled alpine meadows in the early summer and snowfields any time of year. Further south, **Mount St. Helens★★★** is a poignant symbol of nature's power; hikes take in the devastation of the 1980 volcanic blast that carved this landscape as well as its renewal. East of Portland, **Mount Hood★★** is beloved among Oregonians for its scenic summertime hiking trails and wintertime skiing with broad vistas of Cascade peaks. Farther

Bend, Oregon

©Pete Alport/Visit Bend/CCOP

south, in Eastern Oregon, **Mount Bachelor★** offers serene hiking trails in the summer and black-diamond runs with sky-high views in winter.

The region's most famous ski resort is high-profile **Whistler★★★**, north of Vancouver, British Columbia (BC), with 37 lifts and more than 1,000 vertical feet of runs.

AGRICULTURAL BOUNTY

Washington and Oregon have vast agricultural regions producing everything from fruits and cheeses to wines. Both states' wine industries are major economic engines, with award winning wineries tucked amid rolling hills combed by endless vineyards. Wine touring has become a hugely popular pastime. In Washington, most of the grapes are grown in **Eastern Washington**, where climate and growing habits are similar to wine-producing regions in France. The state boasts some 650 wineries, with an industry second only to California. Many wineries in **Washington Wine Country★★** clustered near **Walla Walla★**, and numerous wine tours

11

are available from Seattle. Closer to the city, **Woodinville** is the center of **Western Washington wineries★★**, including the state's oldest, Chateau Ste. Michelle. The center of Oregon's wine country is southeast of Portland, in the northern reaches of the Willamette Valley, around the towns of **McMinnville★**, **Newburg** and **Carleton**, and as far south as the **Ashland★★** area, noted for its year-round **Oregon Shakespeare Festival★★★**.

Among the region's leading agritourism regions are Washington's **Wenatchee Valley**—known for **apple and pear orchards**—and Oregon's **Hood River** area—famed for **fruit orchards** and farms open to visitors, as well as **Sequim**, on the Olympic Peninsula, where **lavender farms★** turn entire landscapes purple in summer. A visit to a farmers' market is the easiest way to experience the region's bounty; all major cities operate weekly farmers markets brimming with regional tastes.

CITY SCENES

A triumvirate of major Northwest cities—**Seattle★★★, Portland★★** and Canada's **Vancouver★★★**—all with scenic waterfronts and major attractions, offer cultural and historical delights. Seattle is a vibrant city situated amid spectacular natural splendor, surrounded by mountains and fronted by the waters of Puget Sound. On the city's waterfront promenade, ferries and tour boats ply the waters. The **Seattle Aquarium★★★** is a destination for families eager to view Northwest sea life, including sea otters. The **Great Wheel** (a new observation wheel) and **Olympic Sculpture Park★** are additional draws, while bustling **Pike Place Market★★★**, a renowned farmers', seafood and crafts market, occupies a hillside overlooking the bay. The **Seattle Art Museum★★★** draws visitors downtown. North of downtown the Seattle Center, with the famous **Space Needle**, attracts concert- and museum-goers to many events and attractions, including the **Chihuly Garden and Glass Museum★**, the **EMP★★** (Experience Museum Project) and **Pacific Science Center★★**. North of town, **Woodland Park Zoo★★★** is among the nation's best.

From the **Hiram M. Chittenden Locks★★**, ocean-going vessels can be seen traveling between a canal and Puget Sound. South of town the **Museum of Flight★★** draws aviation enthusiasts.

Renowned for its green lifestyles, and youthful energy, Portland sits along the Willamette River, near its confluence with the Columbia River. The city's leafy **Cultural District** is home to the **Oregon History Museum★★** and **Portland Art Museum★★**. Evenings theater-goers headto the **Portland Center for the Performing Arts**. A city of neighborhoods, Portland preserves the **Pearl District★** with its boutiques, cafes and the world's largest bookshop, **Powell's City of Books★★**, as well as the **Museum of Contemporary Craft★**. Nearby, Chinatown is home to the exquisite **Lan Su Chinese Garden★★★**. On a western hilltop, **Washington Park★★** holds the **Oregon Zoo★★**, **International Test Rose Garden★★★** and **Japanese Garden★★**.

Just east of Portland, along the Columbia River, the **Columbia Gorge★★** offers dozens of waterfalls, including 620ft **Multnomah Falls★★**. North of Seattle, across the Canadian border, cosmopolitan **Vancouver★★★**, British Columbia, is a multicultural city with a spectacular seaside setting, at the foot of **Grouse Mountain★★**. **Stanley Park★★★**, an immense forested peninsula, is home to the **Vancouver Aquarium★★★**, and its beluga shows. **Granville Island★★** is an arts and shopping hub known for its farmers' market. Totems, face masks and artful carvings at the **UBC Museum of Anthropology★★★** offer insights into the world of First Nations people.

On Southern Vancouver Island, BC's capital city of **Victoria★★★** is known for the stately Edwardian **Empress Hotel★★** overlooking **Inner Harbour★★**, where ferries and float planes pirouette. The **Parliament Buildings★** are lit up at night with thousands of tiny lights. The real spectacle is inside the **Royal BC Museum★★★**: superb collections of First Nations art and artifacts including a **reconstructed big house**. To the north, the extensive formal landscapes of **Butchart Gardens★★** draw garden lovers from around the globe. To the west, **Pacific Rim National Park Preserve★★★** tempts expert hikers from every corner to hike the rugged trail along its wave-lashed beaches and dense forests. Northeast of Victoria, **Gulf Islands National Park Preserve★** beckons water-sports enthusiasts.

Quick Trips

Stuck for ideas? Try these:

IDEAS AND TOURS

13

CALENDAR OF EVENTS

Listed below is a selection of Washington's and Oregon's most popular annual events; dates often vary from year to year. For detailed information on these and other festivals, visit the event websites, contact local tourism offices or see the state tourism websites for Washington www.experiencewa.com or Oregon traveloregon.com.

WASHINGTON EVENTS

Late March–April
Taste Washington
206-667-9463, Seattle,
www.tastewashington.org
Centurylink Field Event Center

April
Skagit Valley Tulip Festival
(All month) 360-428-5959, Mount Vernon, www.tulipfestival.org

Lake April–Early May
Apple Blossom Festival
509-662-3616, Wenatchee,
www.appleblossom.org

April: Skagit Valley Tulip Festival

©Wade Clark Jr.

Early May
Seattle Boat Season
Opening day
206-325-1000, Seattle Yacht Club,
Seattle, www.seattleyacht club.org
Lilac Bloomsday Run
509-838-1579, Spokane,
www.bloomsdayrun.org

Late May
Northwest Folklife Festival
206-684-7300, Seattle Center,
Seattle, www.nwfolklife festival.org
Sasquatch Music Festival
Gorge Amphitheatre, George,
www.sasquatchfestival.com

May–June
Seattle International Film Festival
206-324-9996, Siff Cinema Uptown, Seattle, www.siff.net

Mid-June
Fremont Fair
Fremont Neighborhood, Seattle,
www.fremontfair.org

Late June–August
SeaFair
206-728-0123, Seattle,
www.seafair.com

Mid-July
Sequim Lavender Weekend
360-681-3035,
Downtown Sequim,
www.lavenderfestival.com

Wooden Boat Festival, Port Townsend

©Jan Davis

Late July
Bellevue Arts Fair Weekend
*425-453-1223, Downtown
Bellevue, www.bellevuefest.org*

Labor Day Weekend
Bumbershoot
*206- 673-5060, Seattle Center,
Seattle, www.bumbershoot.org*
Ellensburg Rodeo
*800-637-2444, 609 N. Main
St.,Ellensburg,
www.ellensburgrodeo.com*

Mid-August
Washington State Kite Festival
*360-642-4020, Long Beach,
www.kitefestival.com*
**Vancouver Wine &
Jazz Festival**
*360-906-0441,
Esther Short Park,
Vancouver, WA,
www.vancouverwinejazz.com*

Early September
Wooden Boat Festival
*360-385-3628, Port Townsend,
http://woodenboat.org/festival*

Early October
Issaquah Salmon Days Festival
*425-392-0661, Downtown
Issaquah, www.salmondays.org*

Mid-October
**Dungeness Crab & Seafood
Festival**
*360-452-6300, Port Angeles
City Pier, Port Angeles,
www.crabfestival.org*

Late November–
Late December
Christmas Ship Festival
*206-623-1445, Puget Sound,
Seattle, www.argosycruises.com/
themecruises*

December
Christmas Lighting Festival
*509-548-5807, First three
weekends in December,
Leavenworth,
www.leavenworth.org*

January
Skagit Eagle Festival
*360-853-8784 or 853-8767,
Concrete, www.concrete-wa.com*

15

Playing in Ashland

For more than 75 years the **Oregon Shakespeare Festival** (OSF), a professional repertory theater company, has drawn audiences from around the nation to Shakespearean plays in the cozy, arts-fueled town of Ashland, tucked into rolling hills just 16 miles from the California border. The Tony Award-winning repertory theater produces 11 plays on three stages each season (*Feb-Oct*), including the indoor Angus Bowmer Theatre (600 seats) and Thomas Theatre (360 seats), as well as the gorgeous outdoor Elizabethan Stage (1,190 seats), patterned after London's 1599 Fortune Theatre. Productions include classic and contemporary works, with three to five Shakespeare plays presented each season. The effort expended to put on these plays is immense, with more than 100 actors and many hundreds of support staff and volunteers. Backstage tours offer the opportunity to learn how productions are put on, from costuming to lighting to staging. All told, OSF presents an astounding 750 to 800 plays every year.

OREGON EVENTS

Early May

Taste of the Nation
McMenamins Crystal Ballroom, 1332 W. Burnside, Portland, www.portlandtaste.org

May–June

Portland Rose Festival
503-227-2681, Locations throughout Portland, www.rosefestival.org

Mid-June

Cannon Beach Sandcastle Contest
Cannon Beach, www.cannon-beach.net/cbsandcastle.html

June–September

The Britt Festivals
541-779-0847, Britt Pavillion, Jacksonville, www.brittfest.org

4 July

Waterfront Blues Festival
503-282-0555, July 4 – 7, Tom McCall Waterfront Park, Portland, www.waterfrontbluesfest.com

May–June: Portland Rose Festival

Courtesy Portland Rose Festival Foundation/ Photo by Vern Uyetake

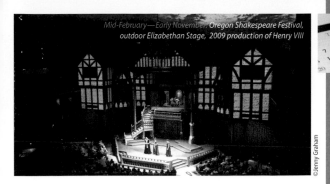

Mid-February—Early November: Oregon Shakespeare Festival, outdoor Elizabethan Stage, 2009 production of Henry VIII

©Jenny Graham

Mid-July
Balloons Over Bend
541-323-0964, Riverbend Park, 799 SW Columbia Road, Bend, www.balloonsoverbend.com

Late July
Oregon Brewers Festival
Tom McCall Waterfront Park, Portland, www.oregonbrew fest.com

Early August
Mount Hood Jazz Festival
Downtown Gresham, www.mthoodjazz.org

August–September
Art in the Pearl Festival
503-722-9017, Northwest Park blocks at NW 8th Avenue, between W Burnside and NW Glisan, Portland, www.artinthepearl.com

Early September
Bandon Cranberry Festival
541-347-9616, Downtown Bandon, www.bandon.com

Mid–September
Pendleton Round-Up
541-276-2553 or 800-45-RODEO, 1205 SW Court Ave., Pendleton, www.pendletonroundup.com

Late September
Feast Portland
Downtown Portland, www.feastportland.com

Late November–December
Christmas Festival of Lights at the Grotto
503-261-2400, 8840 NE Skidmore St. Portland, www.thegrotto.org/christmas

Early December
Portland Revels
503-274-4654, Scottish Rite Center Theater, 709 SW 15th Ave, Portland, www.portlandrevels.org

February
Newport Seafood & Wine Festival
541-265-8801 or 800-COAST44, Rogue Brewery, 2320 OSU Dr. Newport, www.seafoodand wine.com

Mid-February–Early November
Oregon Shakespeare Festival
541-482-2111, Angus Bowmer Theatre, New Theatre, and Elizabethan Stage/Allen Pavilion, Ashland, www.osfashland.org

17

PRACTICAL INFORMATION

WHEN TO GO

The main tourist season for the Pacific Northwest extends from mid-May through September. The Cascade Range creates two different climatic patterns in the region. Moisture moves inland from the Pacific Ocean, producing precipitation mainly in the western half of the region; the interior and eastern parts remain drier and sunnier in summer. Visitors should be prepared for rain at any time of year.

Brief and unpredictable, **spring** brings mild temperatures along the coast and snow in the higher elevations well into late April. It can also bring chilly temperatures at night. Fog, drizzle and rain showers are frequent in spring and fall. Along the coast, **summer** temperatures are mild with highs averaging in the 70s. East of the Cascades, summers are warm and dry with comfortably cool nights. In the higher elevations, snow can block trails, even in July. Rain is minimal in most areas during the summer, when large numbers of visitors flock to the Pacific Northwest. June, July and August are the most rain-free months in the region.

Average Seasonal Temperatures				
	Jan	Apr	Jul	Oct
Portland, OR				
Avg. High	8°C/47°F	16°C/61°F	27°C/80°F	17°C/63°F
Avg. Low	3°C/38°F	7°C/44°F	14°C/57°F	9°C/48°F
Astoria, OR				
Avg. High	10°C/50°F	13°C/56°F	19°C/67°F	16°C/61°F
Avg. Low	3°C/38°F	5°C/41°F	12°C/53°F	7°C/44°F
Salem, OR				
Avg. High	9°C/48°F	16°C/61°F	28°C/82°F	18°C/64°F
Avg. Low	2°C/35°F	4°C/40°F	12°C/53°F	6°C/42°F
Seattle, WA				
Avg. High	8°C/47°F	15°C/59°F	24°C/76°F	16°C/60°F
Avg. Low	3°C/37°F	6°C/43°F	13°C/56°F	8°C/47°F
Olympia, WA				
Avg. High	8°C/46°F	15°C/59°F	25°C/77°F	16°C/60°F
Avg. Low	1°C/34°F	3°C/38°F	11°C/51°F	5°C/47°F
Spokane, WA				
Avg. High	1°C/34°F	14°C/57°F	28°C/83°F	14°C/58°F
Avg. Low	-4°C/25°F	3°C/37°F	13°C/56°F	3°C/37°F

MUST KNOW

Kayaking, Lake Crescent, Olympic National Park

©Russ Veenema

In early September, the spectacular colors of fall are on full display in the higher elevations of Oregon and Washington. Warm, mild weather continues into **autumn** along the coastal sections, but rain and fog occur frequently. Snow arrives early in the higher elevations.

Winter is the stormiest season in the Northwest. While temperatures in the coastal areas rarely dip below freezing, brief storms with high winds bring driving rain and sometimes snow. Seattle and Portland get the majority of their rainfall from October through March. East of the Cascades, winter can begin as early as mid-October, with powdery snow instead of rain transforming the region into a skier's paradise.

No month is completely safe from wet weather. The Cascade Mountains are the ultimate authority on rain. Carving through Washington and Oregon, they form a natural barrier that keeps the western region wetter and greener, while the central and eastern parts of the Northwest enjoy a more arid climate. Check the local forecast at www.weather.com before you go.

Useful Websites

traveloregon.com – Official state tourism website of the Oregon Tourism Commission.

www.experiencewa.com– Official state tourism website of Washington State.

www.visitseattle.org – Official website of the Seattle Convention and Visitors Bureau, with traveler tips including attractions, activities, events, and where to eat and stay.

www.seattle.gov – Official website of the City of Seattle, with comprehensive information and tips for visitors.

www.travelportland.com – Official website of the Portland's Visitor Association, with information on what to see and do, where to eat and stay, events and travel deals.

www.portlandonline.com – Official website of the City of Portland, with a section devoted to visiting Portland.

www.nps.gov/state/wa –
National Park Service information
for Washington State's national
parks.

www.nps.gov/state/or –
National Park Service information
for Oregon's national parks.

www.skioregon.org –
Information about conditions,
events, deals, and even summer
activities at ski areas in Oregon.

www.skiwashington.com –
Comprehensive information about
ski slopes, conditions, resorts and
events in Washington State.

Tourism Offices
Oregon Tourism Association
250 Church St. SE, Ste. 100
Salem, OR 97301, 503-967-1560
traveloregon.com

Washington Tourism Alliance
P.O. Box 953, Seattle, WA 9811,
866-964-8913.
www.experiencewa.com

Local Tourism Offices
Ashland Chamber of Commerce
110 E Main St.Ashland,
Oregon 97520, 541-482-3486
www.ashlandchamber.com
Bend
750 NW Lava Road, Suite 160
Bend, Oregon 97701
541-382-8048, 800-949-6086
www.visitbend.com
Mount Hood
150 Beavercreek Road, Suite 305
Oregon City, Oregon 97045
503-655-8420, 888-622-4822
www.mthoodterritory.com
Oregon Coast
137 NE First St., Newport,
Oregon 97365

541-574-2679, 888-628-2101
www.visittheoregoncoast.com
Portland
1000 S.W. Broadway, Suite 2300
Portland, Oregon 97205
503-275-9750, 800-962-3700
www.travelportland.com
Salem
181 High St. N.E.
Salem, Oregon 97301
503-581-4325, 800-874-7012
www.travelsalem.com
Seattle
701 Pike Street, Suite 800
Seattle, WA 98101
206-461-584; 866-732-2695
www.visitseattle.org
Spokane
201 W Main Avenue
Spokane, WA 99201
509-747-3230, 888-SPOKANE
www.visitspokane.com
Olympia
103 Sid Snyder Avenue SW
Olympia, WA 98501
360-704-7544, 877-704-7500
www.visitolympia.com
Tacoma
1516 Pacific Ave.
Tacoma, WA 98402
253-627-2836, 800-272-2662
www.traveltacoma.com

International Visitors
US Embassies Abroad
In addition to state and regional
tourism offices, visitors from
outside the US may obtain
information from the nearest
US embassy or consulate in their
country of residence *(see partial
list below)*.
For a complete list of American
consulates and embassies abroad,
see the US State Department
Bureau of Consular Affairs listing on
the Internet at travel.state.gov.

- **Australia** – Moonah Place, Yarralumla, ACT 2600; 02 6214 5600; canberra.usembassy.gov
- **Canada** – 490 Sussex Drive, Ottawa, Ontario K1N 1G8; 613-688-5335; canada.usembassy.gov
- **China** – No. 55 An Jia Lou Lu, 100600; 86-10 6532-3000; china.usembassy.gov
- **France** – 2, avenue Gabriel, 85382 Paris Cedex 08; 33 1 43 12 22 22; france.usembassy.gov
- **Germany** – Neustädtische Kirchstr. 4-5, 10117 Berlin, Federal Republic of Germany; 030 2385 174; germany.usembassy.gov
- **Japan** – 1-10-5 Akasaka, Minato-ku Tokyo 107-8420; 03-3224-5000; tokyo.usembassy.gov
- **Mexico** – Paseo de la Reforma 305, Col. Cuauhtemoc, 06500 Mexico, D.F. 01-55 5080 2000 mexico.usembassy.gov
- **United Kingdom** – 24 Grosvenor Square, London W1A 1AE; [44] (0)20 7499 9000 london.usembassy.gov

Entry Requirements

All foreign visitors to the US (including Canadian residents and citizens) must present a valid machine-readable **passport** for entry into the country. Citizens of countries participating in the Visa Waiver Pilot Program (VWPP) are not required to obtain a visa to enter the US for visits of fewer than 90 days. They will, however, be required to furnish a current passport, round-trip ticket and the customs form distributed in the airplane. Travelers from visa-waiver countries who are arriving by air or sea must register at least 10 days

---

Clearing Customs

Persons convicted of a crime or, in some cases, even arrested, may be denied entry to Canada. If in doubt, check with Canadian border authorities before heading to Canada. To bring children into Canada, single parents (whether divorced or simply unaccompanied by their spouse) must bring a notarized permission letter from the other parent, as well as a passport or special enhanced ID.

prior to travel with the Electronic System for Travel Authorization (ESTA) by supplying personal identification information at the US Department of Homeland Security's website, https://esta.cbp.dhs.gov/esta. Citizens of countries not participating in the VWPP must have a visitor's visa. For visa inquiries and applications, contact the nearest US embassy or consulate, or visit the US State Department Visa Services Internet site. travel.state.gov/visa.

Custom Regulations

All articles brought into the US must be declared at time of entry. The following items are **exempt** from customs regulations: personal effects; one liter of alcoholic beverages (providing visitor is at least 21 years old); either 200 cigarettes, 50 cigars (additional 100 possible under gift exemption) or 2 kilograms of smoking tobacco; and gifts (to persons in the US) not exceeding $100 in value. However, it is best if possible not to bring gifts into either the US or Canada, as customs protocols often require search and inspection of gifts.

Prohibited items include firearms and ammunition (if not intended for legitimate sporting purposes); plant materials, meat or poultry products and many other foods. For other prohibited items, exemptions and information, contact any of the following before departure: a US embassy or consulate, U.S. Customs and Border Protection (CBP) Headquarters (US Customs Service, 1300 Pennsylvania Ave. NW, Washington DC 20229; 202-927-1000) or the **US CBP Traveler Information** page on the Internet (www.cbp.gov/xp/cgov/travel). Note that most major cities have a local customs port; contact information is available from Customs Headquarters or from the Internet site. In Washington, customs ports are found in Seattle, border entry cities such as Blaine and Oroville, and ports such as Tacoma. In Oregon, customs ports are found in Portland and ports such as Astoria and Newport. Travelers **crossing into Canada** from the US must likewise declare all items being brought into the country. Note that Canada has stringent gun control laws that strictly regulate the import, for whatever purpose (including hunting or personal protection) of all firearms. Do not attempt to bring guns into Canada. In addition, anyone who has ever been arrested may be denied entry, even if no conviction resulted.

Health

Check with your insurance company to determine if your **medical insurance** covers doctors' visits, medication and hospitalization in the US. If not, it is strongly recommended that you purchase a travel-insurance plan before departing. Many clinics, hospitals, dentists and physicians will not treat walk-in patients—except in emergencies—without cash payment beforehand. Prescription drugs should be properly identified and accompanied by a copy of the prescription.

Safety in the Wild

In most natural areas, tampering with plants or wildlife is dangerous and is prohibited by law. Avoid direct contact with wildlife; any animal that does not shy from humans may be sick.
Some wild animals, particularly bears, may approach cars or campsites out of curiosity or if they smell food. *Never offer food to wild animals—not only is it an extremely dangerous action, it is illegal.*
If a bear approaches, try to dissuade it by talking calmly and backing away slowly. Never approach a mother with cubs, as she may attack to protect her young. Visitors are required to stay 30 yards from a moose and 300 yards from any bear.

GETTING THERE
By Air

Major US airlines serve most of the Northwest's metropolitan areas. Airports with regular nonstop service to and from European cities include **Portland** and **Seattle**. For flight information, contact the airline directly. Numerous US and international airlines fly into Oregon's Portland International Airport and Washington's SEA-TAC Airport, as well as its smaller regional airports.

MUST KNOW

Major Oregon Airports

- **Portland** – Portland International Airport (PDX). 503-460-4040. www.portofportland.com.
- **Eugene** – Eugene Airport (EUG). 541-682-5544. www.flyeug.com.
- **Bend/Redmond** – Redmond Municipal Airport (PDX). 541-548-0646. www.ci.redmond.or.us. (15mi north of Bend)

Major Washington Airports

- **Seattle** – SEA-TAC International Airport (SEA). 206-787-5388. www.portseattle.org.
- **Spokane** – Spokane International Airport (GEG). 509-455-6455. www.spokaneairports.net.
- **Walla Walla** – Walla Walla Regional Airport (ALW). 509 525 3100. www.wallawallaairport.com.

By Bus

Greyhound bus company offers access to most cities and communities. Overall, fares are lower than other forms of transportation, but if you are traveling long distance, there are no onboard sleeping accommodations, and specific seat reservations are not allowed. Advance reservations are suggested. Greyhound offers various discounted online fares (advance purchase) and other specials and promotions; its discount BoltBus service recently began offering service in the Pacific Northwest, with fares as low as $1. For schedules, prices and route information: 800-231-2222 (US only) or www.greyhound.com.

By Train

Amtrak has a nationwide network that serves destinations in most of the states and some Canadian provinces. It is also the only high-speed intercity passenger rail provider in the nation. Amtrak offers discounted fares, regional travel deals, multi-ride tickets and 15-, 30- and 45-day rail passes. For schedules, prices and route information: 800-872-7245 or www.amtrak.com.

By Car

Several Interstate highways offer easy road access to the region. Interstate 5 snakes along the west coast from California up through Oregon and Washington and into Canada. By road, Washington has four **border crossings** into Canada: Blaine/Peace Arch (I 5); Aldergrove (SR 539); Sumas (SR 9); and an auxiliary truck crossing at Blaine right next to I-5. Interstate 90 (I-90) connects 13 states from Boston to Seattle. I-84 and I-82 are also major arteries through the region. The Pacific Northwest's **road system** is well-maintained and open year-round. Visitors should note that snow conditions may affect travel, particularly in the many mountain passes in the region.

By Ferry

Washington State Ferries
(206-464-6400 or 888-808-7977 statewide; www.wsdot.wa.gov/ferries) operates the largest ferry system in the US, with 10 routes serving eight counties within the state and the Canadian province of British Columbia. In Oregon's Wahkiakum County, you can also catch the last remaining ferry service along

the lower Columbia River from Westport, OR to Puget Island, WA (*360-795-3301; www.co.wahkiakum.wa.us*).

GETTING AROUND
By Train
Amtrak provides extensive rail coverage within Washington and Oregon. Its **Cascades Intercity Passenger Rail** service operates between Vancouver, BC and Eugene, OR. In addition, the Washington Department of Transportation (*360-705-7438; www.wsdot.wa.gov/Rail*) operates a commuter light rail line called the **Sounder** (*888-889-6368; www.soundtransit.org*), which runs between Seattle and Tacoma. The Oregon Department of Transportation (*503-986-4321; www.oregon.gov/ODOT/RAIL*) introduced new trains offering service in the Willamette Valley, from Portland to Eugene. **TriMet** (*503-238-7433; http://trimet.org*) provides light rail and commuter rail service within the Portland metro area.

Washington State Ferry on Seattle waterfront

©Tim Thompson/Seattle's Convention and Visitors Bureau

By Ferry
Scheduled ferry service in Washington is provided by the **Washington State Ferries** (*206-464-6400 or 888-808-7977 statewide; www.wsdot.wa.gov/ferries*), which operates the largest ferry system in the US, with 10 routes crossing the Puget Sound and the Strait of Juan de Fuca. While ferries were once a popular means of travel in Oregon, only a handful remain in the state.

By Bus
Oregon has numerous bus routes and services. **Cascades East Transit** (*541-385-8680; www.cascadeseasttransit.com*) offers daily regional transportation service to Bend, La Pine, Madras, Mt. Bachelor, Redmond and Prineville. **Rogue Valley Transportation District** (*541-779-2877; www.rvtd.org*) serves Southern Oregon, with travel to Ashland, Medford, Jacksonville and other cities. **TriMet** (*503-238-7433; http://trimet.org*) provides bus service within the Portland metro area. **Lane Transit District** (*541-687-5555; www.ltd.org*) serves Eugene and Springfield. **Neo Transit** (*541-963-2877; www.neotransit.org*) and **Snake River Transit** (*541-881-0000; www.snakerivertransit.com*) cover eastern Oregon. Smaller bus companies operate in other cities and counties. Similarly, the Washington Department of Transportation (*206-464-6400; www.wsdot.wa.gov/Choices/bus.htm*) oversees various bus fleets throughout Washington State. Statewide travel is facilitated through its **Travel Washington** program, with four lines connecting transit buses with other intercity carriers: The Grape Line offers service

between Walla Walla and Pasco; The Dungeness Line covers the Olympic Peninsula, including Port Angeles, Port Townsend, Seattle and SeaTac International Airport; the Apple Line runs through Omak, Ellensburg and Wenatchee; and the Gold Line connects Colville, Arden, Addy, Chewelah, Loon Lake, Deer Park and Spokane. Public transportation in Seattle is provided by **Metro Transit** (*206-553-3000; http://metro.kingcounty.gov*), and **Sound Transit** (*888-889-6368; www.soundtransit.org*), which operates express buses in Snohomish, King and Pierce Counties.

By Car

Oregon alone boasts more scenic byways than any other state: 25 of the most popular routes are described in www.traveloregon.com. Scenic byways that cover Washington's diverse environments and attractions can be viewed on www.experiencewa.com. Interstate highways and State Roads crisscross this region, offering access to its most remote corners. Oregon also boasts the first **solar highway** in the US, located at the interchange of Interstate 5 and Interstate 205 outside Portland. Check road and weather conditions before you go, as even the summer months can bring hazardous conditions in certain parts of the region. Gas stations become scarcer as you venture farther off the beaten path, so plan accordingly. The Departments of Transportation for Oregon and Washington offer comprehensive information about road conditions and closures.

Rental Cars

National rental companies have offices at major airports and downtown locations. Renters must possess a major credit card and a valid driver's license (international license not required). Minimum age for rental is 25 at most major companies, though younger drivers can often rent by paying a surcharge. All rentals are subject to local taxes and fees which should be included in quoted prices. Liability insurance is not automatically included in the terms of the lease; check for proper insurance coverage, offered at an extra charge. Mileage is usually unlimited (be sure to confirm). Only the person signing the contract is authorized to drive the rental car, but for an additional fee, and upon presentation of the required papers, additional drivers may be approved. If a vehicle is returned at a different location from where it was rented, drop-off charges may be incurred. Most companies offer a fuel-fill option.

Car Rental Companies

* **Alamo** – 800-462-5266 www.alamo.com.
* **Avis**   800-331-1212 www.avis.com.
* **Budget** – 800-527-0700 www.budget.com.
* **Dollar** – 800-800-3665 www.dollar.com.
* **Enterprise**– 800-261-7331 www.enterprise.com.
* **Hertz** – 800-654-3131 www.hertz.com.
* **National** – 800-227-7368 www.nationalcar.com.
* **Thrifty** – 800-331-4200 www.thrifty.com.

PRACTICAL INFORMATION

Recreational Vehicle (RV) Rentals

One-way rentals range from a basic camper to full-size motor-homes that can accommodate up to seven people and offer a bathroom, shower and kitchen with microwave oven. Reservations should be made several months in advance. A minimum number of rental days required. A drop fee is charged for one-way rentals. Cruise America RV (*800-671-8042, www.cruiseamerica.com*) offers rentals with 24hr customer assistance.

The **Recreational Vehicle Rental Association** (RVRA) lists a directory of RV rental locations in the US on their website (*703-591-7130; www.rvra.org*). **RV America** (*www.rvamerica.com*) offers an on-line database of RV rental companies as well as information on campgrounds and RV associations.

Road Regulations

The speed limit on most major highways in Oregon ranges from 55mph (88km/h) to 65mph (105km/h), depending on the location and quality of the road. In Washington, the range is from 60mph (96km/h) to 70 mph (112km/h). (Limits drop within urban areas.) On county roads, the speed limit is usually 50 mph (80km/h). Within cities, speed limits are generally 35mph (56km/h), and average 25-30mph (40-48km/h) in residential areas. Headlights should be turned on when driving in fog and rain. Unless traveling on a divided road, the law requires that motorists in both directions bring their vehicle to a full stop when the warning signals on a school

bus are activated. Parking spaces identified with ♿ are reserved for persons with disabilities only. Anyone parking in these spaces without proper identification will be ticketed and/or their vehicle will be towed.

The use of **seat belts** is mandatory for all persons in the car. Child safety seats are required and are available at most rental-car agencies; indicate need when making reservations. Auto liability insurance is mandatory; if your personal insurance does not cover rental cars, you must purchase coverage from the rental agency. It is illegal to drink and drive and penalties are severe and may include immediate incarceration and surrender of car and driving license.

In Case of Accident

If you are involved in an auto accident resulting in personal or property damage, you must notify the local police and remain at the scene until dismissed. If blocking traffic, vehicles should be moved to the side of the road as soon as possible, unless serious injury has occurred.

Automobile associations such as the **American Automobile Association (AAA)** provide their members with emergency road service. Members of AAA-affiliated automobile clubs outside the US benefit from reciprocal services. Here's a partial list:

- ◆ **Canada** – Canadian Automobile Association (CAA) 613 247 0117
- ◆ **United Kingdom** –
  The Automobile Association (AA) 800 444 999
  The Royal Scottish Automobile Club (RSAC) 141 946 5045

ACCESSIBILITY

The Americans with Disabilities Act (ADA) requires existing businesses (including hotels and restaurants, swimming pools and spa pools) to increase accessibility and provide specially designed accommodations for the disabled. Wheelchair access, devices for the hearing impaired, and designated parking spaces must be available at newly constructed hotels and restaurants.

Many public buses are equipped with wheelchair lifts; many hotels have rooms designed for visitors with special needs. Reservations for hand-controlled rental cars should be made well in advance.

All national and most state **parks** have restrooms and other facilities for the disabled (such as wheelchair-accessible nature trails). Permanently disabled US citizens are eligible for a free **US national recreational lands pass** that entitles the carrier to free admission to all national parks and may provide a 50 percent discount on user fees (campsites, boat launches).

The pass is available at any national-park entrance fee area with proper proof of disability. For details, contact the National Park Service, Office of Public Inquiries (202-208-4747; www. nps.gov). Many attractions also accommodate disabled visitors. For information, contact the **Society for the Advancement of Travel for the Handicapped** (212-447-7284; www.sath.org).

BASIC INFORMATION
Accommodations

For a selection of lodgings in this guide, see Hotels.

Luxury **hotels** are scattered throughout the region, catering equally to travelers who seek chic urban digs, elegant rural retreats or posh accommodations near ski slopes and other popular tourist areas; **motels** tend to cluster on the edges of towns and along major highways. **Bed-and-breakfast inns** usually are found in residential areas of cities and towns, and in more secluded natural areas. Many properties offer special packages and weekend rates that may not be extended during peak summer months (*late May–late Aug*) and holiday seasons, especially near major destinations such as Portland and Seattle. Advance reservations are recommended at all times. Rates are at their peak from May to September; and while winter brings the fewest crowds and best rates, spring and fall also offer their share of deals.

Some cities and communities levy a hotel occupancy tax that is added to hotel rates.

Hotels and Motels

Rates for hotels and motels vary greatly according to season and location, and are much higher during holiday and peak seasons (generally during the summer months). For deluxe hotels, plan to pay at least $200 and up/night per room, double occupancy. Moderate hotels will charge $100–$250/night and budget motels usually charge less than $100/night. In most hotels, children stay free when sharing a room with their parents. In-room efficiency kitchens are available at some hotels and motels. Typical amenities at hotels and motels include television,

Camping near Baker City, Oregon

©Baker County Tourism – Basecampbaker.com

alarm clock, Internet access, smoking/non-smoking rooms and restaurants. Always advise the reservations clerk of late arrival; unless confirmed with a credit card, rooms may not be held after 6pm.

Reservation Services

Hotel reservation services are abundant, especially on the Internet. Here are two.

* **Central Reservation Service** – 800-555-7555. www.reservation-services.com
* **Hotels.com** – www.hotels.com

Camping and RV Parks

Campsites in the Pacific Northwest are located in national parks, state parks, national forests, along beaches and in private campgrounds. Oregon alone has some 500 campgrounds. The season for camping usually runs from May to the end of September; October 1 to April 30 is known as **Discovery Season** in Oregon, a time when you'll find easier access and lower rates at many state campsites. Washington State also has several campgrounds that stay open year-round, particularly along the coast. Some offer full utility hookups, lodges or cabins,

backcountry sites and recreational facilities. Advance reservations are recommended, especially during summer and holidays and at popular locales such as Mount Rainier National Park.

National park and state park campgrounds are relatively inexpensive, but fill quickly, especially during school holidays. Facilities range from simple tent sites to RV spaces or rustic cabins (at most state and national parks and forests, reservations can be made up to six months in advance). Fees vary according to season and available facilities (picnic tables, water/electric hookups, used-water disposal, recreational equipment, showers, restrooms): camping & RV sites $5–$36/day; cabins and yurts $25–$72/day.

For all US national parks, national forests, BLM campgrounds and so on, contact the park you are visiting or the federal reservation site, www. recreation.gov (*518-885-3639 or 877-444-6777; www.recreation.gov*). For state parks, contact Washington State Parks (www.parks.wa.gov) and Oregon State Parks (www. oregon.gov/OPRD/PARKS) for information.

Private campgrounds offering facilities from simple tent sites to full RV-hookups are plentiful. They are slightly more expensive (*$10–$38/day for tent sites, $20–$60/day for RVs*) but may offer more sophisticated amenities: hot showers, laundry facilities, convenience stores, children's playgrounds, pools, air-conditioned cabins and outdoor recreational facilities. Most accept daily, weekly or monthly occupancy. In winter (*Nov–Apr*), many campgrounds are closed. Reservations are recommended, especially for longer stays and in popular resort areas. **Kampgrounds of America (KOA)** operates campsites for tents, cabins/cottages and RV-hookups throughout the US.

For a directory (*order online and pay a $6 shipping or view for free at www.koakampgrounds.com*), contact KOA Kampgrounds, P.O. Box 30558, Billings MT 59114 (*888-562-0000, 406-248-7444*).

Directories of campgrounds throughout the US are easily found on the Internet. Following is a sample of some Internet **campground directories** covering the US:

- **Camping USA** – www.camping-usa.com
- **CIS' RV-America Travel & Service Center** – www.rv-america.com
- **Go Camping America Directory** – www.gocamping america.com
- **Camping.com** – www.camping.com
- **US National Forest Campground Guide** – www.forestcamping.com

Business Hours

Most businesses operate Mon–Fri 9am–5pm. Banks are normally open Mon–Fri 9am–5:30pm; some may have Sat morning hours. Virtually all bank branches big and small, in cities and towns big and small, have ATMs operating 24 hours. Most retail stores and specialty shops are open daily 10am–6pm. Malls and shopping centers are usually open Mon–Sat 10am–9pm, Sun 10am–6pm.

Discounts

Many hotels, attractions and restaurants offer discounts to **senior citizens**, with qualifying ages ranging from 55 to 62 and older (proof of age may be required). Discounts and additional information are available to members of AARP, (*601 E St. N.W. Washington, DC 20049; 202-434-2277, www.aarp.org*), which is open to people over 50.

Electricity

Voltage in the US is 120 volts AC, 60 Hz. Foreign-made appliances may need AC adapters (available at specialty travel and electronics stores) and North American flat-blade plugs.

Emergencies

The emergency phone number throughout the Pacific Northwest is 911, which can be dialed from any operating phone. Visitors in need of urgent non-emergency medical care can visit the emergency room at the closest hospital; or one of many urgent care clinics found in most cities. Patients will likely be required to demonstrate financial ability to pay. Numerous cities in Oregon (Ashland, Eugene, Portland

and Salem, among others) and Washington (Olympia, Seattle and Spokane, among others) have local clinics that provide urgent dental care; and 24 hour pharmacies.

Mail

First-class postage rates within the US are: 45¢/letter (*up to 1oz*) and 32¢/postcard. To Europe: $1.05/letter (up to 1oz) and postcard. Most post offices are open Mon–Fri 9am–5pm; some may open Sat 9am–noon. Companies such as UPS-Mail Boxes Etc. and FedEx Kinko's also provide mail service for everything from postcards to large packages. These companies also sell boxes and other packaging material. For photocopying, fax service and computer access, FedEx Kinko's has locations throughout the US (*800-254-6567, www.fedex.com/us/office/*) or consult the yellow pages in a local phone book under Copying Service for a listing of local companies.

Money

The American **dollar** ($1) is divided into 100 **cents**. A **penny** = 1 cent (1¢); a **nickel** = 5¢; a **dime** = 10¢; a **quarter** = 25¢. Most national banks and Travelex (*locations throughout the US, 800-287-7362, www.travelex.com*) **exchange foreign currency** at local offices and charge a fee for the service. Currency exchange is also available in most major airports, including Portland and Seattle; and at some major banks in large cities.
Other methods to obtain dollars are to use traveler's checks (*usually accepted only in banks and hotels, with presentation of a photo ID*) or to withdraw cash from **ATMs** (Automated Teller Machines) with

a debit or credit card. Banks charge a fee (*$2–$3*) for non-members who use their ATMs. For more information on the ATM network, call MasterCard/Cirrus (*800-424-7787*) or Visa/Plus System (*www.visa.com/atmlocator*). In the event you lose your credit card: immediately call American Express, 800-528-4800; Diner's Club, 800-234-6377; MasterCard/ Eurocard, 800-307-7309; Visa/Carte Bleue, 800-336-8472.
It is also possible to send and receive cash via **Western Union** (*locations in more than 100 countries, 800-325-6000, www.westernunion.com*).

Smoking

The Pacific Northwest and its cities have imposed substantial restrictions on public smoking. Laws vary, but it is illegal to smoke in public areas in most places such as restaurants, airports, buses, and offices open to the public such as banks and retail stores.
Some hotels in the region, including a few large chains, still offer smoking rooms.
Aside from legal restrictions, it is socially unacceptable to expose other individuals to tobacco smoke. Virtually all smokers voluntarily retire to locations where their habit will not affect others.

Taxes and Tipping

Although Oregon has **no sales tax**, the state of Washington has a **sales tax** of 6.5 percent, with some cities adding an additional tax. Some cities and counties in both states also collect a hotel/motel tax. In restaurants, it is customary to leave the server a gratuity, or **tip**, of 15–20 percent of the total bill (since it almost never is included otherwise). Taxi drivers are generally tipped 15 percent of the fare. Hotel bellhops and courtesy bus drivers are tipped $1-$2 and housekeeping $1-$2 per night.

Telephones

For **long-distance** calls in the US and Canada, dial 1 + area code (3 digits) + number (7 digits). Note: Many cellular phones, depending on the service provider, do not require the initial 1; just dial the 10-digit number you wish to call. To place **local calls**, dial the seven-digit number without 1 or the area code, unless the local calling area includes several area codes. To place an **international call**, dial 011 + country code + area code + number. To obtain help from an **operator**, dial 0 for local and 00 for long distance. For **information** on a number within your area code, dial 411. For long-distance information, dial 1 + area code + 555-1212. To place **collect calls**, dial 0 + area or country code + number. At the operator's prompt, give your name. For all **emergencies**, dial **911**.

Since most **hotels** add a surcharge for local and long-distance calls, it is preferable to use your calling card or cell phone. Local calls from public telephones cost 50¢ unless otherwise posted. **Public telephones** accept quarters, dimes and nickels and credit cards. You may also use your calling card or credit card (recommended for long-distance calls to avoid the inconvenience of depositing large amounts of change). Instructions for using public telephones are listed on or near the phone.

Important Phone Numbers	
Emergency (police, fire department)	☏911
Directory Assistance	☏411

Toll-free - The telephone area codes for Washington are 206, 253, 360, 425 and 509; in Oregon, area codes are 458, 503, 541 and 971. Unless otherwise indicated, telephone numbers that start with **800, 888, 877** and **866** are toll-free within the US, and often Canada. European travelers may find that their phone service provider does not offer connection to US toll-free numbers; if so, call the direct number (beginning with the area code for that city) instead. Numbers that begin with 900 charge extra fees, sometimes exorbitant; do not use these.

Time Zones

Most of the Pacific Northwest is in the Pacific Time Zone, which is three hours earlier than New York; a small area of eastern Oregon is in the Mountain Time Zone, which is two hours earlier than New York. Daylight Saving Time is observed from mid March to mid-November; time is moved forward one hour, bringing a later dawn but also a later dusk. Pacific Standard Time (PST) is 8hrs behind Greenwich Mean Time (GMT).

PRACTICAL INFORMATION

NORTHWEST WONDER

Comprised of the US states of Washington and Oregon, as well as southern British Columbia in Canada, the Pacific Northwest is a vast region encompassing the northwest corner of the continental US and lower western Canada. Covering approximately 167,000sq mi, it's close to the same size as California (163,707sq mi). The Northwest is marked by an astonishing diversity of geology, topography and ecosystems. Its saltwater shorelines run from the forested Pacific Ocean coasts of British Columbia south along the wave-washed beaches of Washington and Oregon. From the Pacific to Washington's and Oregon's glacial peaks to the sagebrush flats of the Columbia Basin, east of the Cascade Range, the region brims with great natural beauty—as well as wildlife, from bears and eagles to whales and sea lions. The region is renowned for its abundance of outdoor recreational opportunities; within the Pacific Northwest are 20 national parks and monuments.

Visitors and locals are drawn to the coasts, mountains and deserts for whale-watching off the **San Juan Islands**, hiking amid wildflowers on **Mount Rainier** or exploring the volcanic landscapes of Eastern Oregon. Oregon's **Mount Hood** features one of the continent's longest ski seasons, while Washington's **Mount Baker** boasts the highest average snowfall of any ski resort, worldwide. Combined, Washington and Oregon host a population topping 10 million residents, many extremely protective of their state's spectacular natural environments; the bustling cities of **Portland** and **Seattle** are well known for their efforts to minimize pollution and urban sprawl. Northwesterners are justifiably proud of the treasure trove of natural resources and untrammeled beauty they have in

Fast Facts Oregon

Land area: 98,380 sq mi.

Population: 3.9 million

Capital city: Salem

Largest city: Portland (population 594,000; metro area 2.2 million)

Record temperatures: hottest 119˚F (Aug 10, 1898); coldest -54˚ F (Feb. 10, 1933)

Average annual precipitation: 75 inches (coast); 51 inches (west of Cascades); 12 inches (eastern).

Annual days of sunshine: 68 (Portland); 117 (eastern)

Fast Facts Washington

Land area: 66,456 sq mi.

Population: 6.8 million

Capital city: Olympia

Largest city: Seattle (population 620,000; metro area 3.5 million)

Record temperatures: hottest 118˚F (Aug 5, 1961); coldest -48˚ F (Dec. 30, 1968)

Average annual precipitation: 142 inches (coast); 39 inches (Seattle); 15 inches (eastern).

Annual days of sunshine: 51 (coast); 71 (Seattle); 109 (eastern)

their backyard, forged over eons
before mankind set foot here.
Glacial handiwork left U-shaped
valleys, fjords—including **Puget
Sound** in Washington State
and along western **Vancouver
Island**—and sharp and broken
ridges atop mountain ranges. In
Oregon, glacier-mantled 11,253ft
Mount Hood rises just east of
Portland. To the north, across the
Columbia River, volcanic **Mount
St. Helens** (8,365ft), which erupted
in 1980, reveals the awesome
power of nature. Seattle residents
prize their view of nearby Mount

Rainier, a 14,410ft behemoth
whose snow-topped shoulders
take on peach-colored hues at
sunset. The Cascade range is high;
seven of the peaks reach skyward
10,000ft, rivaling the Rockies.
The region's earliest inhabitants
revered the volcanic mountains
and other landscapes, orally
passing down rich creation myths
about the coyote, beaver, raven,
whale, and other creatures that
inhabited their world. More than
15,000 years ago, mankind's
inquisitive nature must have
prompted humans to cross a land

*Mount St. Helens eruption,
May 18, 1980*

©U.S. Geological Survey

bridge over the **Bering Strait** from what is now Siberia. By 8,000 years ago, they migrated far enough south to witness the eruption of Mount Mazama in the Oregon Cascades. The **Coast Salish** people thrived along the complex waterways of Washington and British Columbia, and tribes such as the **Nez Perce**, **Cayuse**, **Modoc** and **Yakama** lived on high plateaus east of the Cascades. The first Europeans to arrive were probably the crew of Spanish explorer **Juan Rodriguez Cabrillo**, whose ship reached the mouth of Oregon's Rogue River in 1543. To the north, Russian fur hunters began forays along the coast in the mid-1700s, reducing the sea otter population by millions before the fur trade declined. When **Lewis and Clark** reached their journey's end at the mouth of the **Columbia River** in 1805, it opened the way for **Oregon Trail** pioneers to settle the gentle **Willamette Valley**. In 1807 Britain's Hudson's Bay Company set up trading posts in Washington, and in 1811 Yankee trader **John Jacob Astor**

established Fort Astoria on the coast of Oregon. By the 1860s the Northwest's plentiful bowhead whales, and later humpback whales and even walruses, were slaughtered for the lamp-oil market. In 1850 gold was discovered in Oregon, and in 1855 gold was found in the Colville area of Washington, and along British Columbia's Fraser River. The Yakama, **Spokane**, **Palouse** and **Coeur d'Alene** tribes were forced to cede 6 million acres of their traditional land to the US government. When land they'd been compensated with was encroached on by prospectors, they banded together to resist the trespassing and attendant violence. In what became known as the **Yakama War**, the US army hung 24 tribal chiefs and killed hundreds of tribal horses.

In 1897 a gold-laden ship from Alaska's Klondike docked in Seattle, causing a stampede to the city, the launch point to the Yukon; businesses sprang up overnight, and the city ballooned. In the mid- to late 19C blacks,

Haystack Rock, Cannon Beach, Oregon

©Leslie Forsberg/Michelin

Oregon's Green Ways

One of the first state's to pass legislation to preserves natural resources, Oregon was the first state to encourage **recycling** of bottles and cans through refunds. A leader in **clean energy**, it supplies wind- and water-generated power to other Western states. It's positioned at the cutting edge in emissions reduction, with efficient transportation systems, including a light-rail connection between Portland International Airport and downtown. Portland's **green buildings** include eco-roofs and other energy-saving innovations. Even many of the parking meters in the city are solar-powered. In Willamette Valley, many of the state's vineyards are certified as sustainable, organic or biodynamic, conserving the health of natural resources. Oregon Tilth, a research organization that works to ensure biologically sound agriculture, is known worldwide as the certifying body for organic growers and processors.

Japanese, Chinese and Hawaiians who arrived to work in the railroad and timber industries were denied civil rights, and anti-Chinese sentiments grew during an economic depression in the 1880s. Laws were enacted to exclude Chinese immigrants, and in 1885 whites attacked the Chinese, forcibly expelling them and burning their homes and businesses. World War II brought the forced imprisonment of all Americans of Japanese descent from coastal communities. Founded in Seattle in 1916, the **Boeing Airplane Company** created regional employment for 50,000 workers during World War II, and was Washington's primary employer for decades. Oregon remained the nation's leading **timber-producing** state until the 1950s. World Fairs in Portland and Seattle promoted economic expansion, and helped forge Seattle's reputation as a portal to the Pacific Rim and Canadian markets.

Today, despite the recent economic downturn, Washington's $15 billion and Oregon's $8.8 billion **tourism** industry continue to expand. Visitors can access superb museums and historical sites. Festivals, farmers' markets, theaters and concert halls showcase regional arts and culture. Urban and even small-town restaurants and nightspots are usually crowded. **Coffeehouses** and cafes abound. Eco-friendly excursions, scenic drives, picturesque vineyards and wine tours, as well as shopping opportunities, offer enjoyable outings. Outdoor adventurers hop on a bike, paddle a kayak or put mileage on their hiking boots.

A premier destination for winter-sports enthusiasts, the soaring peaks of the Northwest are a playground for alpine and cross-country skiers, snowboarders, snowmobilers, snowshoers and sledders. And when precipitation falls in the form of rain, as it no doubt will, visitors can duck into a city bookstore or a museum and happily pass the time until the sun reappears, as it no doubt will.

NATIONAL PARKS

From the snowbound, 14,411ft summit of Mount Rainier to the expanse of wilderness beach at Olympic National Park, the Northwest's national parks embrace the region's natural splendors. Cathedral-like groves of old-growth forest—among the last remaining in the US—line tumbling rivers in Rainier, Olympic, North Cascades and Crater Lake parks. The latter's volcanic caldera holds North America's deepest lake, a 1,943ft caldera of sapphire-blue waters. Elk, deer, bears, eagles and falcons prowl the woods and soar in the skies of these famous parks; salmon throng their rivers and streams. In British Columbia, Pacific Rim National Park Reserve is a coastal strip of Sitka spruce forest and strands of golden sand. Gulf Islands National Park preserves an island ecosystem unique in the world. All these famous preserves hold the natural treasures uniquely characteristic of the region, and have beckoned adventurers for more than a century.

CRATER LAKE NATIONAL PARK★★★

80mi northeast of Medford on Rte. 62. Open daily year-round. $10/vehicle. 541-594-3000. www. nps.gov/crla. Steel Visitor Center open late Apr–early Nov daily 9am–5pm; rest of the year daily 10am–4pm; closed Dec 25. Rim Visitor Center open late May–late Sept 9:30am–5pm.

Crater Lake National Park

©Chrisboswell/Dreamstime.com

Crater Lake (elevation 1,932ft) is the world's deepest volcanic lake. The sapphire-blue lake rests in the basin of a collapsed volcano, surrounded by steep-walled cliffs. **Wizard Island**, a volcanic cinder cone, rises at its west end. Ringed by mountains tinged with snow much of the year, the 6mi diameter lake attracts hikers and sightseers from around the world. The lake—so renowned for its clarity that its water has set new standards for water purity—was formed when the cataclysmic eruption of Mount Mazama 7,700 years ago created a bowl-shaped caldera that filled with snowmelt. One of the most scenic drives in the world, 33mi loop **Crater Rim Drive★★★** has more than 20 overlooks, but there are ample other attractions here as well, including hikes through mid-elevation pine forests, and the famed **boat tour★★** to Wizard Island.

Rim Drive circles the lake allowing spectacular **views**. Among the best are those from **Sinnott Memorial Overlook**★★ *(Rim Village, south side of lake)* and **Cloudcap**★★, highest point on the drive (7,865ft). Better yet is the perspective from atop 8,929ft **Mount Scott**★★, requiring a strenuous 5mi round-trip hike to the park's highest summit. A 7mi spur road off Rim Drive leads to **The Pinnacles**★, where hollow, fossilized fumaroles reach up to 80ft in height. The historic (1915) **Crater Lake Lodge**★★ *(closed in winter; 541-594-2255; www. craterlakelodges.com)* is one of the most atmospheric park lodges in the country. Perched on the crater rim, the lodge features rustic ambiance in public spaces and modern accommodations; many rooms have peerless views.

MOUNT RAINIER NATIONAL PARK★★★

Open daily year-round. www.nps. gov/mora. $15/vehicle. Paradise Visitor Center open Jun–Sept daily 10am–5pm; rest of the year Sat–Sun only, hours vary. Access Paradise via Nisqually-Paradise Rd., Rte. 706 (road open year-round; all other roads closed late-Oct–late Jun, depending on snow). Free Sat–Sun shuttle (Jun–Sept) to Paradise from Ashford; also from Longmire and Cougar Rock.

On clear days, the majestic, 14,410ft glaciated crown of the highest mountain in Washington rises high above the Puget Sound region, visible at startling distances. The highest volcano and fifth-highest peak in the contiguous US, Rainier is an arctic island in a temperate zone; the summit is covered with more than 35sq mi of ice and snow. Meltwater from its 26 glaciers filigrees the terrain with waterfalls and fast-running rivers and streams that course through flower-carpeted alpine meadows in summer. At the mountain's lower reaches, ancient forests harbor massive old-growth Douglas-fir, hemlock and Western red-cedar trees.

Mount Rainier National Park

©lawdawg1/Flickr.com

Named by Capt. George Vancouver in 1792, and successfully climbed in 1870 by two Olympia men, Rainier was ascended in 1888 by conservationist **John Muir**, whose writings about the peak's splendors sparked public interest. In 1899 Mount Rainier was established as the nation's fifth national park. Within are five developed areas, three of which are described below. **Ohanapecosh**, in the park's southeast corner, is not accessible in winter; its visitor center is open seasonally *(Jun–early Oct)*. The northwest area, **Carbon/Mowich**, is historically subject to flooding, and vehicle access is limited.

Paradise★★★

The park's main access point, at the southwest corner, is 19.5mi east of the Nisqually Entrance.

The most popular area in the park is famed for wildflower meadows and spectacular mountain views. The park's main visitor center, **Paradise Jackson Visitor Center**, is here, as is the 1916 **Paradise Inn**, with its rustic lodge rooms and large public spaces. Snowshoeing, Nordic skiing and tubing are favorite winter activities; in summer the world-class 5.5mi **Skyline Trail** to Panorama Point is busy with hikers. The equally beautiful **Nisqually Vista Trail** *(1.2mi)* offers similar scenery in a smaller dose.

Sunrise★★★

Closed in winter. 14mi west of White River entrance.

Sitting at 6,400ft at the northeast edge of the mountain, Sunrse is the highest point in the park reachable by vehicle. The **Sunrise Visitor Center** provides an introduction to the mountain's history and the surrounding flora and fauna. Several **trails** through meadows here are home to marmots, a burrowing rodent with a piercing whistle. The Sunrise area permits fantastic **views★★** of Rainier's **Emmons Glacier**, as well as of other volcanoes in the Cascade chain.

Grove of the Patriarchs★★

Near the Stevens Canyon entrance, off Rte. 123.

At the mountain's southeast edge, a trail *(1mi round-trip)* leads to a **small island** in the Ohanapecosh River. There rises a stand of towering old-growth trees, some as old as 1,000 years and some measuring 50ft in circumference.

Longmire★

Closed in winter. 6.4mi northeast of Nisqually Entrance.

Situated in the southwest corner of the park, this National Historic District centers on the rustic **National Park Inn**. Housed in the former park headquarters building (1916-28), the compact **Longmire Museum** offers exhibits on natural history and the area's past. The **Wilderness Information Center** provides guidance to visitors interested in hiking, climbing or camping. Trails from here are snow-free earlier in the season than elsewhere in the park.

NORTH CASCADES NATIONAL PARK★★

Open daily year-round. www.nps. gov/noca. Visitor center on Rte. 20, Milepost 120, near Newhalem; 206-386-4495; open early May– late Oct daily 9am–5pm (6pm Jul–early Sept).

The **North Cascades Highway★★** (*State Rte. 20*) is the northernmost passageway through the Cascade Mountain Range in Washington, and the only highway that runs through the National Park. Closed in winter, the scenic byway begins at Interstate 5, just north of Mount Vernon, and rambles alongside the **Skagit River**, flanked by dense forests of Douglas-fir and cedar. As it ascends, the road passes through several hamlets before entering the park, a stunning, 500,000-acre wilderness where massive granite peaks tower overhead, more than 300 glaciers cling to cirques and 127 alpine lakes glimmer in the sun. Despite its astonishing sights, this park is one of the least-visited in the nation, largely

North Cascades National Park

©National Park Service

due to inaccessibility. The park's boundaries do not reach the highway, and there is no paved road into the park. Visitors must hike roughly an hour, for example, just to reach the popular **Cascade Pass** hiking trail. Most who do visit the park merely enjoy the **view** while driving over the pass.

OLYMPIC NATIONAL PARK★★★

Open daily year-round. 360-565-3131. www.nps.gov/olym. $15/ vehicle. Main visitor center (3002 Mt. Angeles Rd., Port Angeles) open mid-Jun–mid-Sept daily 8:30am–6pm; rest of the year hours vary. Park access: US-101 encircles the perimeter; spur roads branch off to scenic highlights; no roads access the interior.

A UNESCO World Heritage Site and an International Biosphere Reserve, this 922,000-acre park embraces

wildflower-strewn meadows tucked among glacier-cloaked peaks; ancient, moss-covered trees in rain forest valleys; and miles of remote Pacific Ocean beaches. Indigenous peoples hunted here for thousands of years. It wasn't until 1890 that an expedition, led by James Christie, crossed the Olympics from the strait to the ocean. In 1909 President Theodore Roosevelt created the Mount Olympus National Monument.

The National Park was established in 1938; it protects some 73mi of coastline and temperate rain forests as well as more than 300 species of birds and 70 species of mammals, among them, Roosevelt elk *(see Hoh Rain Forest below)*.

Hurricane Ridge★★★

17mi south of park visitor center via Hurricane Ridge Rd.

Nearly a mile in elevation, paved 17mi Hurricane Ridge Road climbs through dense, old-growth fir forests, looping around knolls and past grottos where waterfalls cascade off snowy slopes. Glaciated peaks rise around the ridge top, and the towns of Port Angeles and Sequim spread out below, the Straits of Juan de Fuca and Vancouver Island visible beyond.

In summer the high meadows burst with colorful wildflowers, and alpine firs take on bonsai-like forms, contorted by winter snows. Black-tailed deer forage the lowlands and the whistles of Olympic marmots echo off the hillsides. **Meadow Loop Trail**, near Hurricane Ridge Visitor Center, offers a gentle introduction to the mountain environment, and 1.5mi **Hurricane Hill Trail** is popular, though its steep drop-offs are not for the faint of heart. Myriad wildflowers line nearby 5mi **Mount Angeles Trail**. In winter a small ski operation and weekend **guided snowshoe walks** offer family fun.

Pacific Coast Beaches★★★

Large colonies of nesting seabirds inhabit the western Olympic Peninsula coastal bluffs and islets, which are protected by three national wildlife refuges and the Olympic Coast National Marine Sanctuary. Sea stacks dot the horizon 12mi west of Forks at rocky **Rialto Beach**, on the north side of the Quillayute River; a 1.25mi trail here leads to the "Hole in the Wall." Farther north, in the Quileute Nation reservation, **First Beach** is known for its colorful wave-washed pebbles and its regular wave sets that draw surfers. Two national park beaches—2mi-long **Second Beach** and mile-long **Third Beach**—lie south of here, reachable by short trails; both are wild and scenic, with driftwood

Hurricane Ridge, Olympic National Park

©Russ Veenema

Freeing the Elwha

The **Elwha River**, coursing from the Olympic Mountains to the Straits of Juan de Fuca, was hobbled by two immense dams for nearly a century, allowing salmon access to only the lower 5mi of the 45mi-long river. The aging 108ft **Elwha Dam** was removed in spring 2012, and the 210ft **Glines Canyon Dam** will be gone by the summer of 2013. Their demolition allows all five species of Pacific salmon to return to their spawning grounds. The dam removal project is the world's largest, with the equivalent of more than 24million cu yds of sediment trapped behind the two dams and subsequent 70ft-deep barren silt flats challenging re-vegetation. A short **trail** to an overlook near the start of Highway 112 affords views of the former Elwha Dam site, where the muscular teal-shaded waters flow freely again.

jumbles, sea stacks and tide pools. **Ruby Beach★** (off Hwy. 101) edges the southwest coast of the Olympic Peninsula; it has sea stacks and plenty of space for beachcombing. The climb over piles of driftwood to reach the beach is worth it. South 9mi, broad, sandy beaches mark **Kalaloch★★** (pronounced "clay lock"); it has two campgrounds, a ranger station (open daily in summer), picnicking facilities and nature trails. The venerable **Kalaloch Lodge** (www.visitkalaloch.com) offers accommodations; its restaurant serves excellent clam chowder. **Lake Ozette** (off Hwy. 112, south of Neah Bay; ranger station at its entrance) offers access to 57mi of coastal wilderness. Two 3mi trails here lead to **Sand Point** and **Cape Alava**. Between the two points, at Wedding Rocks, **petroglyphs** were left by early inhabitants.

Lake Crescent★ and Sol Duc Hot Springs★

Tucked inside steep ridgelines 18mi west of Port Angeles, **Lake Crescent★** is a sapphire-hued, glacially carved lake renowned for its clarity. Highway 101 traverses the curvy south side of the 9mi-long lake, offering spectacular **views★★**. Hiking trails radiate off the lake, including one to **Marymere Falls★**, which starts at the Storm King Ranger Station, (off Hwy. 101) and meanders through a Douglas-fir and maple forest less than a mile to the falls, which tumble 90ft into a fern grotto. The 4mi-long **Spruce Railroad Trail** hugs the northern shore of the lake. Several day-use picnic areas dot the lakeshore, and a campground, Fairholme, sits at the west end. The 1915 **Lake Crescent Lodge★** (416 Lake Crescent Rd., 360-928-3211) is a popular base for outdoors enthusiasts; rowboats are available for rent here.

Just 2mi west of Lake Crescent, a road heads through dense forest to the **Sol Duc Hot Springs★** (open Apr–mid-Oct; 866-476-5382), where two mineral-laden hot **soaking pools**, a wading pool, and a large freshwater pool as well as rustic cabins await visitors. The smell of sulfur lingers in the air here, and the setting is sublimely relaxing. The lovely .7-mi trail to nearby **Sol Duc Falls★** passes through old-growth Douglas-fir forest.

NATIONAL PARKS

41

Rain Forests

With as much as 14ft of rain per year, the peninsula's western valleys roar with the sound of rivers tumbling from glacier fields, carving their way through rain forests of primeval western hemlocks, Douglas-firs, Sitka spruce and big-leaf maple. In this emerald-green world, moss covers everything that doesn't move. Despite the peninsula's soggy reputation, most of the precipitation occurs during the fall and winter; summer can be dry and pleasant. The park's two temperate rain forests—the Hoh and Quinault—each have a visitor center, trails, campgrounds and picnic areas; ranger-led programs are available in summer.

Situated 91mi southwest of Port Angeles, the **Hoh Rain Forest★★★** offers an introduction to this vibrant ecosystem. You might catch a glimpse of the park's famous **Roosevelt elk**, which make their home in the Hoh River Valley. Three nature **loop trails** near the **Hoh Rain Forest Visitor Center** *(360-374-6925)* reveal fern glades beneath mammoth trees garbed with layer upon layer of epiphytes.

About 53mi south of the Hoh, **Quinault Rain Forest★★** surrounds 8.5mi-long, 1,000ft-deep **Lake Quinault**. The lake's north shore lies within the National Park; its south shore is part of the Olympic National Forest. The 31mi **Quinault Rain Forest Loop Drive** takes in the lake and both parks, with waterfalls and nature trails en route, including a 1.3mi loop to the Kestner Homestead, and a path winding through groves of big-leaf maples. The 1926 **Lake Quinault Lodge★** *(360-288-2900, www.visitlakequinault.com)*, a grand structure with a massive brick fireplace, enjoys a prime location on the south shore of the lake; the Roosevelt Dining Room serves regional specialties such as cedar plank salmon and halibut. On North Shore Road the **Quinault Rain Forest Ranger Station** *(360-288-2444)* offers park maps and information.

PACIFIC RIM NATIONAL PARK RESERVE★★★

West side of Vancouver Island. Hwy. 1 north from Victoria to Parksville, Hwy. 4 west through Port Alberni to the park. 250-726-7721.www.pc.gc.ca. Open daily year-round, but park facilities are closed mid-Oct–mid-Mar. $7.80.

Wave-tossed rocky headlands, long sand beaches, deep old-growth spruce forests and an inland sound with untouched islands are some of the natural elements that make up this natural preserve. Hugging the west coast of Vancouver Island, this Canadian National Park includes three distinct units: Long Beach, Broken Group Islands and West Coast Trail. The park's **visitor center** *(open mid-Mar–mid-Oct daily 9am–6pm; 250-726-4212)* is located just past the junction where Highway 4 turns north. **Long Beach★★** – Stretching from just north of Ucluelet in the south *(where Hwy. 4 turns north)* northward to within 4.8km/3mi of **Tofino**★, this area is the only part of the park reachable by a road. The namesake beach has almost 32km/20mi of shoreline, most of it open beach, with firm, gray sand for strolling, dozens of offshore sea stacks that send waves crashing upward, and open expanses where breaking waves draw hordes of surfers (Tofino is widely regarded as the surfing capital of Canada).

Radar Hill★★ – About 29km/18mi north of the visitor center, the 300ft summit (highest on this stretch of coast) of this hill affords a 360-degree **panorama**★★ of the ocean and the island behind. The road ends in Tofino, 33.5km/21mi from the Ucluelet junction.

Broken Group Islands – The second unit, composed of more than 100 islands, is contained entirely within **Barkley Sound,** a small inland sound south of Ucluelet. It is one of the premier **saltwater kayaking** areas on earth.

Pacific Rim National Park Reserve
©Leslie Forsberg/Michelin

West Coast Trail – This legendary 75km/47mi wilderness trail traverses the coast between Bamfield and Port Renfrew. The arduous trek takes up to six days, the weather is notoriously temperamental, and reservations are necessary long in advance, as park officials limit yearly use to about 8,000 hikers.

GULF ISLANDS NATIONAL PARK RESERVE★

Open daily year-round. 250-654-4000. www.pc.gc.ca. Visitor center at 2220 Harbour Rd., Sidney; open year-round Mon–Fri 8am–4:30pm.

Established in 2003, Canada's new reserve spreads across 15 of the Gulf Islands, encompassing 35sq km/13.5sq mi of numerous discrete pockets of island preserves inland and on the shore; and 26sq km/10sq mi of marine habitat. Many of these islands can be reached only by boat. One of the most interesting islands is **Russell Island**, a small islet near Salt Spring that was homesteaded by immigrant native Hawaiians around the turn of the 20C. Guided **kayak trips** to Russell Island are led by **Island Escapades** *(250-537-2553; www.island escapades.com).*

SEATTLE ★★★

With a population of 620,000 residents, the largest city in Washington anchors the west-central part of the state. Flanked by snow-cloaked mountains—the Olympics to the west, the Cascades to the east, Mount Rainier to the south—and the waters of Puget Sound at its feet, Seattle is a center for outdoors enthusiasts. Lakes and canals add to the Emerald City's al fresco charms. The vibrant, world-class metropolis has cultivated its own brand of healthful living in recent decades. Seattleites live primarily in single-family dwellings, recycling and cycling to work, and cultivating backyard gardens, complete with chickens. With an abundance of Northwest seafood and produce from nearby farmlands, the city's regional cuisine has vaulted a number of local restaurants to national fame.

MUST SEE | SEATTLE

Coast Salish peoples roamed the shores of what's now **Elliott Bay** long before British naval captain George Vancouver sailed into **Puget Sound** in 1792. No serious settlement occurred in the area until the 1850s, when an Oregon Trail party chose Alki Point as a suitable site. Chief **Sealth** and his fellow Duwamish Indians welcomed the newcomers. Eventually a trading post and lumber mill were established, and throughout the late 1850s, Seattle continued to grow. With local timber depleted, coal became the city's major export. In 1897 Seattle became the gateway to the Klondike, supplying gold

Fast Facts

Incorporated: 1869

Land area: 92 square miles

Population: 620,000 (city); 3,492,000 (metro)

Days of sunshine a year: 71

Average annual precipitation: 38.6 inches

Distance to Canadian border: 111 miles

prospectors who swarmed the city. As the gold petered out, timber barons **Frederick Weyerhaeuser** and **William Boeing** established industries that would fuel the area's economy for years to come

Seattle sklyine

©Tim Thompson/Seattle's Convention and Visitors Bureau

Practical Information

When to Go

Seattle isn't known for sun, but it's normally sunny and dry from early July through early October, with an average temperature of 76°F in July and August. October through May is the rainy season; average annual rainfall is 38 inches.

Getting There and Around

◆ **By Air – Sea-Tac International Airport** (SEA) (206-787-5388; www.portseattle.org) is the primary airport for the Seattle region; the airport has rental-car agencies and connects to public transportation. Central Link light rail trains *($2.75)* run every 7.5min–15min between Sea-Tac Airport and Westlake Station in downtown Seattle; the trip takes 37min.

◆ **By Train – Amtrak** (800-USA-RAIL; www.amtrak.com) provides daily service from Chicago, Los Angeles and Vancouver, BC, stopping at many other stations en route. **SoundTransit** (888-889-6368; www.soundtransit.org) provides commuter rail service between Seattle, Everett and Tacoma.

◆ **By Bus – Metro Transit** (206-553-3000; metro.kingcounty.gov) provides bus service throughout the city.

◆ **By Car** – There's no need for a car when staying in downtown Seattle, but a vehicle is necessary for excursions. Interstate-5 runs north-south through downtown, separating the downtown from Capitol Hill. Street parking *($4/hr)* for up to 2hrs is available in the city center, with **automated pay stations** that accept credit cards; parking lots are plentiful. Parking is free after 8 pm and on Sundays and holidays.

◆ **By Taxi – Yellow Cab** (206-622-6500; www.yellowtaxi.net), **STITA** (206-246-9999; www.stitataxi.com) and **Orange Cab** (206-522-8800; www.orangecab.net)

Visitor Information

The **Seattle Visitors Bureau** (206-461-5800; www.visitseattle.org) offers a wealth of information about things to see and do while in the city. **Visitor centers:** Washington State Convention Center, 7th Ave. & Pike St. (206-461-5840). Pike Place Market at First Ave. and Pike St. (206-461-5840).

(Boeing switched from timber to a new technology: flight). Early 20C streetcar suburbs expanded city boundaries, drawing German, Scandinavian, Italian and Asian immigrants as workers and entrepreneurs, but the bombing of Pearl Harbor in 1941 prompted authorities to send the city's 7,000 Japanese residents to detainment camps. The early 1960s brought construction of **I-5** and Seattle's second **World's Fair,** and now famous icon, the Space Needle. The fair structures left behind formed the basis for a major urban renewal project. The latest such project will renovate the city's waterfront. Home to Starbucks and lots of roasteries (plus high-tech giants Microsoft and Amazon), Seattle has a widespread cafe culture. It's known for sparkling seascapes and recreational opportunities.

SEATTLE

NEIGHBORHOODS

Downtown★★

Seattle is sophisticated and bustling, yet it still manages to exude a small-town feel. The city's **waterfront promenade**, along Alaskan Way, is a major draw for locals and visitors alike. Here, ferries carry passengers to nearby **Bainbridge Island**, a plethora of seafood restaurants offer outdoor seating, and parks lend themselves to enjoying the glittering views. Pier 52, at the south end of the waterfront, is the **Washington State Ferries** terminal, where ferries depart to Bainbridge Island and the Olympic Peninsula, beyond. Miners' Landing, at Pier 57, with an arcade and carousel, is the home of the Great Wheel, a 175ft Ferris wheel with gondola cars. At Pier 59, the **Seattle Aquarium** offers views of sea life found beneath the waters of Puget Sound and along the Pacific Coast, from coiled octopi to playful sea otters and sleek sea lions. Outdoor **Olympic Sculpture Park** (see Parks and Gardens) sits at the northern edge, and adjacent **Myrtle Edwards Park★** is a lovely shoreline greenway with a 1.25mi walking path and pocket sand beach.

The city's venerable and beloved **Pike Place Market**, one of the oldest farmers' markets in the nation, with crafts booths and numerous restaurants, steps down a hillside overlooking the waterfront. Victor Steinbrueck Park, overlooking Elliot Bay at the north end of the market, features one of the best waterfront **views**. Off the waterfront, **Benaroya Hall**, home to the Seattle Symphony, is a major cultural hub, and the adjacent **Seattle Art Museum** boasts an excellent collection of African art, as well as Northwest Coast Native artworks. Just south of downtown, gallery-filled **Pioneer Square** has a lively bar scene that becomes even more active when games let out in the adjacent **SoDo District** sports complexes.

Seattle Center★★

North of downtown, at the base of Queen Anne Hill, Seattle Center draws millions annually for its performing-arts scene, museums, concerts and festivals. This lively, 74-acre park and cultural center was originally the setting for the 1962 World's Fair, formally called

---

Coast Salish Experience

Argosy Cruises (206-682-8687; www.tillicumvillage.com) offers one of the region's most cherished cultural experiences, an opportunity to experience traditional Coast Salish Native American life, on its **Tillicum Village** excursion. This cultural attraction on nearby **Blake Island**, a half-hour boat ride from downtown, treats visitors to plank-roasted salmon, followed by a contemporary theatrical production that showcases the origins and culture of Coast Salish tribes. While waiting for the return boat, guests are welcome to explore the sand beaches and forested trails of the 475-acre island, where curious deer often greet visitors.

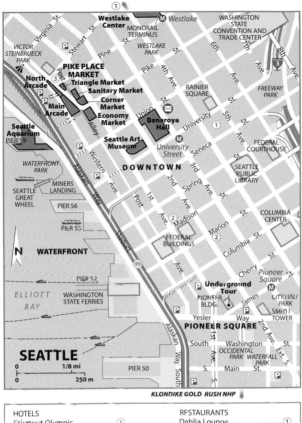

KLONDIKE GOLD RUSH NHP

HOTELS		RESTAURANTS	
Fairmont Olympic	①	Dahlia Lounge	①
Hotel 1000	②	Metropolitan Grill	②
Inn at the Market	③		

the Century 21 Exposition. The 605ft-high **Space Needle★★**, a historic landmark built during the fair, is the center's most-prominent feature, drawing out-of-towners and locals alike to best-in-the-city **views** from atop its **observation deck★★** and **SkyCity**, a rotating restaurant.

At the base of the Needle, the new (2012) **Chihuly Garden and Glass Museum** (see Museums) is dedicated to the colorful works of the world-famous glass artist Dale Chihuly, an area local.

McCaw Hall, at the northern edge, is the home of **Pacific Northwest Ballet**, known for its unique, Maurice Sendak-designed staging of The Nutcracker every holiday season, and **Seattle Opera**, which produces Richard Wagner's Ring Cycle every four years. Several theaters reside on

Space Needle and EMP Museum

© Tim Thompson/Seattle's Convention and Visitors Bureau

the Seattle Center grounds, as well as several museums, including the architecturally dramatic **EMP** (Experience Music Project), which pays tribute to the Northwest's rich rock music history, and the superb, interactive **Seattle Children's Museum**★ (206-441-1768; www. thechildrensmuseum.org). Kids are also drawn to the **Pacific Science Center**★★, with its interactive science exhibits, IMAX theater and tropical butterfly house.

International District★

This colorful ethnic neighborhood east of Pioneer Square is home to Chinese, Filipino, Japanese, Vietnamese and Southeast Asian families. Most businesses in this district are small and family owned. Whole roast ducks hang in barbecue joint windows and baskets of Asian vegetables spill onto the sidewalk next door to ethnic eateries. **Uwajimaya**★, an immense grocery and general-goods store with an ethnic-inspired food court, stocks an eclectic assortment of imports. The **Wing Luke Museum of**

the Asian Pacific American Experience (see Museums) illuminates the history of Asian immigration to the Northwest. At South King Street and 5th Avenue South, the elaborate **Chinatown Gate** marks the western entrance of old Chinatown, and nearby **Hing Hay Park** (423 Maynard Ave. S.) has a fire-engine-red Grand Pavilion. The district hosts festivals throughout the year, from the Lunar New Year (Jan) to Bon Odori and the Dragon Fest, both in July.

SoDo District

South of Pioneer Square, SoDo boasts **Century Link Field**, home turf for NFL's **Seattle Seahawks** (www.seahawks.com) and soccer league's **Seattle Sounders FC** (www.soundersfc.com). Next door, **Safeco Field**★ hosts the MLB **Seattle Mariners** (www. seattlemarinersmlb.com), who play in the American league.

Fremont★

North of downtown, across the Lake Washington Ship Canal, Fremont (www.fremont.com) is the self-avowed Center of the Universe, a quirky, artsy neighborhood with sights you'll never see anywhere else, such as the **Fremont Troll★★**, a colossal public artwork beneath the Aurora Bridge; the hairy beast actually clutches a real Volkswagen Beetle. Nearby, a 16ft bronze **statue** of Vladimir Lenin *(600 N. 36th St.)* rescued from obscurity following the fall of the Soviet bloc is a startling relic that draws attention outside a gelato shop *(N. 34th St. and Evanston Ave. N.)*, and a 1950s Cold War **rocket fuselage** a block south is pointed spaceward on the side of a building, as if ready to blast off at any moment. Fremont is every bit an alternative venue, with funky second-hand and collectibles shops, clothing boutiques, tiny international eateries, coffee shops and bakeries. Among the neighborhood's top draws is **Theo Chocolate** *(3400 Phinney Ave. N.; 206-632-5100; www.theochocolate.com)*, which roasts organic, Fair Trade cocoa beans to create rich truffles and uniquely flavored chocolate bars; popular **factory tours★** of the huge brick factory come complete with plenty of samples.

The **Fremont Sunday Market** draws visitors from throughout the region to buy produce and peruse crafts, and the **Fremont First Friday Art Walk** offers yet more crafts and artworks. This freewheeling community puts on the Northwest's most unique festivals, ranging from the **Moisture Festival** *(late Mar –mid-Apr)* to the **Solstice Parade** *(late Jun)*, known for its anything-goes displays, including (unauthorized, yet perennial) naked bicyclists with artfully applied body paint.

Ballard

Situated 5mi northeast of downtown Seattle, across the Ballard Bridge, this traditional Scandinavian community was originally known for its fishing fleet. In recent years Ballard has shifted gears, transforming itself from a sleepy suburb into a high-profile dining and nightlife center increasingly surrounded by high-rise condos. Vestiges of Ballard's Nordic past remain, such as the cheery **Scandinavian Specialties** gift shop on 15th Street; the **Nordic Heritage Museum★**, with its display of Nordic immigration and traveling exhibits; and the annual **Syttende Mai** (Norwegian Constitution Day) parade on May 17, but today Ballard is better known for wine bars than Nordic wares.

When dusk falls, most of the action takes place in the **Ballard Avenue Historic District★**, home to a galaxy of trendy cocktail bars and restaurants, several of them spotlighted on the national stage. On Sundays, this same stretch of the neighborhood is taken over by the **Ballard Farmers' Market★★**, one of the best in the city. Reminiscent of the community's seafaring past, the **Hiram M. Chittenden Locks** *(see Historical Sites)*, west of downtown Ballard, is one of the best free attractions in the city. Here, seagoing or lake-bound vessels rise or fall to the level of Puget Sound or the ship canal. The surrounding **Carl S. English, Jr. Botanical Garden** makes a tranquil spot for strolling.

MUSEUMS

EMP Museum★★

325 Fifth Ave. N. at Broad St. 206-770-2700. www.empmuseum.org. Open late May–early Sept daily 10am–7pm (til 5pm in winter). $20.

The **Experience Music Project**'s psychedelically colored building by visionary architect Frank Gehry pays tribute to the rock 'n 'roll musicians who helped shape Seattle's music scene. Highlights include nods to Seattle music icons **Jimi Hendrix** and **Kurt Cobain**. Co-founder Microsoft billionaire Paul Allen's fascination with sci-fi was the impetus for the museum's **Science Fiction Hall of Fame**, in which temporary exhibits honor the works of leading sci-fi creators.

MOHAI★★

860 Terry Ave. N. 206-324-1126. www.seattlehistory.org. Open year-round daily 10am–5pm (til 8pm Thu). $14.

The **Museum of History and Industry** (MOHAI) is dedicated to exploring the region's history, from wilderness roots to the world spotlight. In late 2012 it moved to a spacious new facility, the former Naval Reserve Building at the south end of Lake Union. Showing first-person interviews of past and present community members, the **Prologue/Epilogue Theater** is the cornerstone of the museum.

Seattle Art Museum★★★

1300 First Ave. 206-654-3100. www.seattleartmuseum.org. Open year-round Wed–Sun 10am–5pm, (Thu–Fri til 9pm). $17, free first Thu each month.

This expansive museum with more than 23,000 objects does a particularly fine job of showcasing ethnic art. Significant holdings of arts and crafts include those from Korea, Japan and China; African ceremonial masks and headdresses; and Northwest Coast basketry and wood sculptures. Traditional European paintings and sculpture, as well as modern art, are also represented.

Seattle Asian Art Museum★★

1400 E. Prospect St., in Volunteer Park. 206-654-3100. www.seattle artmuseum.org. Open year-round Wed–Sun 10am–5pm (til 9pm Thu). $7, free first Thu each month.

Housed in an Art Moderne building in a park atop Capitol Hill, the museum boasts one of the top collections of art outside Asia,

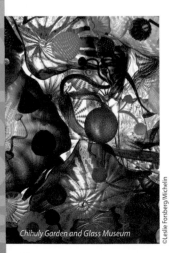

Chihuly Garden and Glass Museum

©Leslie Forsberg/Michelin

with more than 7,000 objects. The meditative space holds South Asian Buddhist and Hindu sculpture, 4,000-year-old Chinese vessels and finely wrought Japanese ceramics and temple art.

Burke Museum of Natural History and Culture★

University of Washington campus, 17th Ave. NE and NE 45th St. 206-543-7907. www.burkemuseum.org. Open year-round daily 10am–5pm. $10, free first Thu each month.

The diverse geology, archaeology and ethnology of the Pacific Rim are showcased on two exhibit floors. The lower level features artifacts and photographs that highlight cultures of the Northwest Coast, the Pacific Islands, and East and Southeast Asia. Main-floor exhibits illuminate the geologic past with dinosaur skeletons, mineral specimens and an exhibit on plate tectonics.

Chihuly Garden and Glass Museum★

305 Harrison St. 407-956-3527. www.chihulygardenandglass.com. Open year-round daily 11am–7pm (til 8pm Fri–Sat). $19.

An homage to Tacoma-born glass artist **Dale Chihuly** (b.1941), the museum is housed at the Seattle Center. Inside, a universe of red-, orange- and yellow-colored glass sculptures brighten the **Glasshouse**, a glass-walled structure; the artworks glow when the sun's rays light them up. Eight art-glass galleries, a whimsical garden of glass delights and a cafe add to the charms of this new (2012) museum.

Frye Art Museum★

704 Terry Ave. 206-622-9250. www.fryemuseum.org. Open year-round Tue–Sun 10am–5pm (til 7pm Thu).

This gem of a small museum features 19C and 20C representational paintings by American, French and German artists that are the legacy of 19C art collectors Charles and Emma Frye. Among the permanent collection are works by Albert Bierstadt, Winslow Homer and John Singer Sargent. In recent years the museum has expanded its range to include contemporary installations and works by world artists.

Wing Luke Museum of the Asian Pacific American Experience★

719 S. King St. 206-623-5124. www.wingluke.org. Open year-round Tue–Sun 10am–5pm (til 8pm first Thu and third Sat). $12.95.

This Smithsonian Institution affiliate is the only museum in the nation dedicated to the Asian Pacific American experience, including an unflinching look at 19C Chinese immigrant oppression and WWII Japanese imprisonment. Tours take in the historic **Yick Fung Mercantile**—a well-preserved company store—and a hotel that once served as a home for new arrivals. **Honoring Our Journey** *(2nd floor)* is the centerpiece exhibit, devoted to themes such as Getting Here, Making a Living and Social Justice.

HISTORICAL SITES

Pike Place Market★★★

First Ave. and Pike St. 206-682-7453. www.pikeplacemarket.org. Open year-round daily 9am-6pm (til 5pm Sun); individual shop and restaurant hours differ.

The market's 9 acres and dozen of buildings are protected in a national historic district; city residents voted overwhelmingly in 1971 to preserve this slice of Seattle, which was threatened with development in the 1960s. Often called the soul of Seattle, the Pike Place Market (frequently and mistakenly called "Pikes" Place Market) was built in 1907. Fun and infinitely appealing, with buskers adding to the colorful atmosphere, the market offers an abundance of local foods, including farm-fresh berries, seafood and flower bouquets, and some of the best restaurants in the city can be found here. A vsit to the market is always visually arresting; Pike Place Fish vendors toss fish to one another over the heads of gawkers, and across the street, Beecher's Handmade Cheese has view windows overlooking vats of churning cream.

Hiram M. Chittenden Locks★★

3015 NW 54th St. 206-783-7059. www.nws.usace.army.mil.

The U.S. Army Corps of Engineers oversees the two locks here, built in 1917 to link the Lake Washington Ship Canal with Puget Sound. Visitors flock to the locks to 🚶 **watch the procession** of boats—pleasure and fishing craft, freight and research vessels—tie up and rise or fall before passing through gates into the canal or sound. On the south side, past rushing spill gates atop a dam, a **fish ladder** with viewing windows enables salmon to bypass the locks while visitors watch them. Flanking the waterway is the **Carl S. English Jr. Botanical Garden** and visitor center.

Pike Place Market sign

Klondike Gold Rush National Historical Park★

Pioneer Square, 319 Second Ave. S. 206-220-4240. www.nps.gov/klse.

The small museum has interactive exhibits and artifacts detailing the Yukon Gold Rush and its impact on the city, beginning when the steamship *Portland* arrived on July 17, 1897, with two tons of gold. Summer interpretive programs include **gold-panning demonstrations** and ranger-led tours of historic Pioneer Square.

Pioneer Square

Bounded by Cherry and S. King Sts., Alaskan Way and Fourth Ave. S. 206-667-0687. www.pioneersquare.org.

Filled with late 19C brick and stone buildings and shaded by trees, historic Pioneer Square anchors the south end of downtown. The site of Seattle's first permanent settlement, the district today is brimming with bars and clubs, restaurants and galleries. The square's **First Thursday Seattle Art** Walk is the city's largest and

Tlingit Indian totem pole, Pioneer Square

©Tim Thompson/Seattle's Convention and Visitors Bureau

oldest such event. At night Pioneer Square's boisterous nightclubs spring to life. *(It's best not to walk alone here after dark.)* The 38-story **Smith Tower★** (*506 Second Ave.; 206-622-4004; www.smithtower. com*), built in 1914, was the tallest building on the West Coast until the Space Needle was erected in 1962. The tower's **Observation Deck** (*$7.50*) offers panoramic **views★★** of the city and Mount Rainier.

History still reigns supreme in the Seattle unit of **Klondike Gold Rush National Historical Park** (*see above*), as well as the popular Bill Speidel's **Underground Tours★★** (*206-682-4646, www. undergroundtour.com*), which descend into tunnels—the original street level of Pioneer Square—in which visitors learn colorful details about Seattle life from the mid-19C through Prohibition. **Pioneer Place** (*First Ave. and Yesler Way*) is marked by a 1930s Tlingit Indian **totem pole**.

Happy Trails

With the waterfall-laden Cascade Range an hour's drive east of Seattle and the snow-crested Olympic Range 2 hours west, Seattle is a perfect home base for day hikes. To learn more about the hundreds of miles of scenic trails throughout the state, visit the **Washington Trails Association's** hiking guide database at www.wta.org.

FOR KIDS

Woodland Park Zoo★★★

Phinney Ave. N. 206-684-4800. www.zoo.org. Open May–Sept daily 9:30am–6pm. Rest of the year daily 9:30am–4pm. $17.75, $11.75 children.

Covering 92 acres, this world-class zoo is highly acclaimed for its conservation ethic (the zoo is home to 35 endangered species) and naturalistic habitats. It offers dynamic glimpses of 1,100 animals engaged in natural behavior: grizzly bears fish for trout in a stream on the **Northern Trail**, orangutans shimmy up trees in **Trail of Vines**, zebras dash about in **African Savanna**, and jaguars peer warily from behind a kapok tree in **Jaguar Cove.**

Pacific Science Center★★

200 Second Ave. N. 206-443-2001. www.pacificsciencecenter. org. Open year-round Mon–Fri 9:45am–5pm (til 6pm Sat–Sun). Closed Tue Sept–May. $16, $11 children (ages 6-15).

Grizzly bear, Woodland Park Zoo
©Ryan Hawk/Woodland Park Zoo

The center's graceful arches soar skyward adjacent to the south end of Seattle Center. Inside six interconnected buildings, a maze of interactive exhibits include the new "Professor Wellbody's Academy of Health and Wellness," with a Fitness Play Zone. Also at the center are **robotic dinosaurs**, a **laser dome**, two **IMAX theaters** and a tropical **butterfly house**.

Center for Wooden Boats★

1010 Valley St. 206-382-2628. www.cwb.org. Open late Apr–early Sept Tue–Sun 12:30pm–8pm. Rest of year Sat–Sun only; hours vary.

A living museum of more than 100 historic boats on Lake Union, this center preserves the Northwest's maritime heritage. Visitors can rent **vintage sailboats or rowboats** to ply the waters of the lake; children can rent **pond boats** *(Sun 11am–2pm)*, and anyone can stroll the docks admiring the well-kept old-time vessels. The center also hosts concerts (think sea shanties) and boat-building classes.

Pacific Science Center
©John Keatley/Pacific Science Center

SEATTLE

MUST DO

THE GREAT OUTDOORS

Green Lake★★

6 mi north of downtown, between Aurora Ave. N. and I-5. 206-684-4075. www.seattle.gov/parks.

This recreational lake and green space is beloved by Seattle residents. Thousands visit it daily to stroll, skate or jog its 2.8mi **loop path★★**. The park is a natural preserve witvh hundreds of species of trees and plants; many birds and waterfowl are commonly found here, including red-wing blackbirds in the spring. The park's community center has an indoor **swimming pool**, as well as two **bathing beaches** with lifeguards on duty seasonally. A small-craft center rents **paddleboats and sailboats** for those so inclined, yet most choose to just enjoy a picnic on the lakeshore while watching the endless array of action.

Alki Beach★

Alki Ave. SW. 206-684-4075. www.seattle.gov/parks.

The city's first settlers, the **Denny Party**, spent the winter of 1851 on Alki Beach before moving to the site of today's Pioneer Square. The views of the downtown skyline and Puget Sound from here are among the best in the city. In summer the sand attracts sunbathers and volleyball players, and the 2.5mi **beachfront promenade★** is a hot spot for roller bladders, joggers and others who come here to enjoy the outdoors and then find a spot in a beachside cafe to watch the passing parade. The **King County Water Taxi** *($3.50; www.alkiferry.com) runs between* Pier 50 downtown, and Alki *(every half-hour Mon–Fri and hourly Sat–Sun).*

Lake Cruises

Cruises on Seattle's Lake Union and Lake Washington are given by **Argosy Cruises** *(206-622-8687; www.argosycruises.com)*, the city's chief day-cruise operator, and **Waterways** *(206-223-2060; www.waterwayscruises.com)*.

View of Seattle from
Seacrest Park, West Seattle

©Leslie Forsberg/Michelin

PARKS AND GARDENS

Bellevue Botanical Garden★

12001 Main St., Bellevue. Open daily dawn–dusk. 425-452-2750. www.bellevuebotanical.org.

East of Lake Washington, this 53-acre preserve focuses on plants that thrive in the Pacific Northwest. Colorful cultivated gardens include the Dahlia, Native Discovery, and Fuchsia gardens, as well as woodlands and wetlands.

Discovery Park★

3801 Discovery Park Blvd. 206-386-4236. www.cityofseattle.net/parks.

This 534-acre expanse on Magnolia Hill, a former military property, is the largest city park in Seattle. Situated atop a bluff overlooking Puget Sound, an **old-growth forest★** and **West Point Lighthouse★**, the park offers fine **views★★** of the Sound and the Olympic Mountains. Hikers and joggers use a 3mi **loop trail★** through wooded ravines, past old-

growth maple trees. Families build driftwood forts on the beach.

Olympic Sculpture Park★

2901 Western Ave. at Broad St. 206-654-3100. www.seattle artmuseum.org.

This 9-acre outdoor park, overlooking Elliott Bay holds a representative collection of large-scale sculptures by Calder, Serra, Nevelson and Oldenburg. Views from the park are lovely.

Rhododendron Species Botanical Garden★

24mi south of Seattle. 2525 S. 336th St., Federal Way. 253-838-4646. www.rhodygarden.org. Open year-round Tue–Sun 10am–4pm. $8.

Washington State's flower is the rhododendron, and there's no place better to see them in bloom *(Mar–May)* than at this 22-acre woodland garden: 10,000 rhododendrons add brilliance to a serene conifer forest.

Washington Park Arboretum★

2300 Arboretum Dr. E. 206-543-8800. www.depts.washington. edu/uwbg.

Preserving 230 acres of woodlands, the arboretum is the legacy of landscape-architect brothers John and Frederick Law Olmsted Jr., who laid out its gardens in the early 20C. The **Japanese Garden★** *(206-684-4725; www.seattle.gov/parks)* is a meditative space fashioned around a pond with willows.

Bellevue Botanical Garden

©Todd Medley

PERFORMING ARTS

BOX OFFICE

Benaroya Hall★★

200 University St. 206-215-4800.
www.seattlesymphony.org.

Occupying an entire downtown city block, Benaroya Hall is the home of the Seattle Symphony as well as regional performing arts groups. Opened in 1998 with two performing halls, the venue played a part in revitalizing the city's downtown core.

Marion Oliver McCaw Hall★★

321 Mercer St. 206-733-9725.
www.seattlecenter.com

The result of a major renovation of the Seattle Opera House, the city's premier performance venue opened in 2003. The hall's auditorium seats 2,900 for performances by the **Pacific Northwest Ballet** (*206-441-2424, www.pnb.org*) and the **Seattle Opera** (*206-389-7676, www.seattle opera.org*), as well as the **Seattle Men's Chorus** (*206-388-1400, www.flyinghouseproductions.org*).

5th Avenue Theatre★

1308 5th Ave. 206-625-1900.
www.5thavenue.org.

This jewel box of a theater, built as a vaudeville palace in 1926, has a Chinese motif, with gold-leaf embellishments and a dragon painted on the ceiling. Home to touring Broadway shows, the theater also has a resident non-profit theater company that stages its own productions that have traveled on to Broadway.

Teatro Zinzanni★

222 Mercer St. 206-802-0015.
www.zinzanni.org.

This theater got its start in Seattle in 1998, and the concept—equal parts circus, dinner theater and zany mayhem—continues to enthrall visitors. The three-hour experiential performances combine five-course dinners with improv comedy, cabaret, dance, aerials and more. Each performance evolves into a production that's never quite the same each night, thanks to audience participation. Three new shows are staged each year.

ACT Theatre

700 Union St. 206-292-7676.
www.acttheatre.org.

With two main-stage theater spaces, including a theater-in-the-round, each seating 390 guests, ACT Theatre productions have an intimate feel to them. The company, known for cutting-edge productions, has had many national and West Coast premieres.

Seattle Repertory Theatre

155 Mercer St. 206-443-2222.
www.seattlerep.org.

This venerable theater company has premiered plays by August Wilson, Neil Simon, John Patrick Shanley and Wendy Wasserstein, among others. Located at the Seattle Center, with two theater spaces, the Rep offers classics, recent Broadway hits and new works.

PERFORMING ARTS

SHOPPING

Downtown

At the heart of downtown, **Westlake Center** (*400 Pine St., 206-467-1600, www.westlakecenter. com; see downtown map*) is a 4-story, glass-fronted shopping mall with a top-level food court as well as the southern terminus for the **monorail**, which transports passengers between downtown and the Seattle Center.

The city's retail core fans out from **Westlake Park**, outside Westlake Center, with the flagship **Nordstrom** store to the east and Macy's to the west. Numerous national-brand shops are situated along **Pike and Pine Streets** and along **5th Avenue and 6th Avenue**.

Pacific Place★ (*6th Ave. and Pine St.; 206-405-2655; www. pacificplaceseattle.com*) is the hot spot for upscale shopping, dining and entertainment. Here some 50 shops range from Ann Taylor to Williams-Sonoma, the AMC Pacific Place contains 11 movie theaters and nearly a dozen restaurants offer Asian, Italian, Mexican or other fare.

University Village

2623 NE University Village St. 206-523-0622. www.uvillage.com.

This charming open-air shopping center northeast of downtown features a distinctive collection of **national-brand stores** such as Crate & Barrel, The Gap and Banana Republic, and Northwest boutique shops like the deservedly popular **Fran's Chocolates**. With sculptures and fountains along an interior courtyard, a children's play area and charming boutiques, "U Village" has a relaxing ambiance.

Westfield Southcenter

2800 Southcenter Mall, Tukwila. 206-246-7400. www.westfield.com/southcenter.

The largest shopping mall in the Pacific Northwest, Westfield Southcenter is situated in Tukwila, four miles east of Sea-Tac International Airport. The massive mall was renovated in 2008. It features 188 stores, including major and local retailers, and numerous restaurants.

Westlake Center

©Tim Thompson/Seattle's Convention and Visitors Bureau

NIGHTLIFE

🛇 Century Ballroom

915 E. Pine St. 206-324-7263.
www.centuryballroom.com.

Few spaces can match the Century
Ballroom for elegance and Old
World flair. Every night of the week,
classes and dances ranging from
salsa and swing to tango and waltz
draw hundreds to this palatial
dance hall. The floor, at 2,000sq ft,
is one of the largest in the city, and
the facility includes a full bar and
restaurant for those who wish to
make a night of it.

🛇 Dimitriou's Jazz Alley

2033 Sixth Ave. 206-441-9729.
www.jazzalley.com.

Jazz Alley is the city's premier
live-music jazz venue, drawing
international jazz artists ranging
from Diane Schuur to Taj Mahal.
With a balcony overlooking the
action, there's not a bad seat in the
house. A state-of-the-art sound
system ensures excellent acoustics,
and concert-goers can dine on
Northwest fare at the in-house
restaurant as they enjoy the show.

Showbox at the Market

1426 First Ave.
www.showboxonline.com.

Founded in 1939, the Art Deco-
style Showbox has introduced
city residents to a broad sweep of
musical styles over the decades,
from the Jazz Age to the grunge era.
Touring acts and local talent playing
here have included bands ranging
from Duke Ellington to Pearl Jam.
The Showbox books a lively mix of
200 diverse concerts a year.

🛇 Triple Door

216 Union St. 206-838-4333.
www.thetripledoor.net

The Triple Door, a dinner theater,
lounge and music venue that
completely transformed a former
vaudeville theater, features plush,
half-moon booths, a state-
of-the-art sound system and
sophisticated decor. The venue,
which books folk, indie and World
Music bands, is one of Seattle's
best live-music spaces. The on-site
restaurant, Wild Ginger, is among
the city's top Asian restaurants.

©Century Ballroom

Century Ballroom

EXCURSIONS

Snoqualmie Falls★★

Off I-90, 29mi east of Seattle;
6501 Railroad Ave SE, Snoqualmie.
www.snoqualmiefalls.com.

The waters of the Snoqualmie River
dash 270ft over a massive rock
ledge and into a basalt basin a half-
hour east of Seattle at Snoqualmie
Falls. This famous waterfall is at the
top of the area's list of attractions,
especially following rainy periods,
when the falls swell tremendously.
Beside the falls, **Salish Lodge &
Spa** is a luxury destination with
a cliff-top view of the falls and
a renowned restaurant serving
Northwest specialties.

Bainbridge Island★

*Due west of Seattle, across Puget
Sound. Accessible by Washington
State Ferries from Pier 52 (35min
one-way).*

A spectacular salt-air **ferry ride**
takes visitors to the Island, beloved
for its quaint downtown, quiet
country lanes and gardens and
parks. The island's main town,
Winslow, is a 5min minute from
the ferry. The compact, lively town

Raingear Refusal

Seattleites pride themselves
on never using umbrellas, so
if you spy a soggy passerby,
it's likely he or she is a city
native.

is filled with boutiques, jewelry
shops and excellent restaurants, as
well as a famed ice-cream parlor,
Mora Iced Creamery★.
In the late 19C and early
20C, Japanese farmers grew
strawberries in vast fields across
the island; on a side street
downtown, the **Bainbridge
Island Historical Museum** *(215
Ericksen Ave. NE; 206-842-2773;
www.bainbridgehistory.org)*
showcases the island's history.
Today Bainbridge is known for its
public gardens, the most famous
is 150-acre **Bloedel Reserve★★**
*(7571 N.E. Dolphin Dr.; 206-842-
7631; www.bloedelreserve.org; open
Jun–Aug Tue–Wed 10am–4pm,
Thu–Sun 10am–7pm; rest of the
year Tue–Sun 10am-4pm; $13)* with
showy formal gardens surrounding
a pond and estate home.

Japanese guesthouse, Bloedel Reserve

MUST SEE SEATTLE

Bellevue★

*Across Lake Washington, a 9mi
drive from Seattle via I-90. www.
visitbellevuewashington.com*

The well-heeled mini-metropolis
of Bellevue (pop.122,000) boasts
vaunted restaurants and the
largest concentration of retail
shops in the region, including
🚶 **The Bellevue Collection★**,
*(bounded by NE 4th and NE 10th,
100th Ave. NE and 106th Ave. NE;
425-454-8096. www.thebellevue
collection.com)*, a cluster of high-
end shopping centers.
The **Bellevue Arts Museum★**
*(510 Bellevue Way NE, Bellevue;
425-519-0770; www.bellevuearts.
org; open Tue–Sun 11am–5pm; $10,
first Fri/ month free)* focuses on
Northwest art, crafts and design
in rotating exhibits. Bellevue's
performing arts center, the
Theatre at Meydenbauer Center
*(425-450-3810; www.meydenbauer.
com/theatre)* is the home of the
Bellevue Opera.
The 53-acre **Bellevue Botanical
Garden★** *(12001 Main St.; 425-452-
2750; www.bellevuebotanical.org;
open daily dawn–dusk)* preserves
cultivated gardens, woodlands and
wetlands.

Kirkland

5mi north of Bellevue via I-405.

North of Bellevue, Kirkland is a
haven for shoppers, with charming
boutiques and colorful **galleries**
lining leafy streets along Lake
Washington. Swanky restaurants,
including waterfront eateries,
can be found here, as well as the
Kirkland Performance Center
(425-828-0422; www.kpcenter.org),
which presents national artists

Berry Tasty

Berries grow like weeds
in Seattle's mild maritime
climate, and in summertime
most restaurants serve up
delectable berry treats, but
in July you can pick your
own delicious (non-native)
blackberries in the city's
natural parks.

ranging from Jane Monheit to
Philip Glass. To best experience
Kirkland take a Lake Washington
Argosy Cruise *(206-623-1445;
www.argosycruises.com)*; **tours★**
permit views of waterfront
mansions, including Bill and
Melinda Gates' colossal hillside
home.

Woodinville

*18mi northeast of Seattle
via Rte. 522.*

The verdant Sammamish River
Valley contains more than 90
wineries★★ clustered alongside
country lanes that parallel the
Sammamish River. The town of
Woodinville boasts the luxurious
Willows Inn★★ and the legendary
Herbfarm Restaurant★★ —an
early adherent to the local foods
movement that draws guests from
around the world. The venerable
Chateau Ste. Michelle, which
opened in 1976, was the catalyst
for the growth of Washington's
wineries. *For more information
about Woodinville Wine Country, see
www.woodinvillewinecountry.com
or www.gotastewine.com.*

CRUISES FROM SEATTLE

With two cruise-ship terminals and ships departing nearly every day, Seattle is the West Coast's key departure port for **Alaska cruises**, which operate May through September during the Northwest's best weather window. The best time to cruise weather-wise is July and August, yet the entire cruise season offers spectacular snowy views, breaching whales and plunging waterfalls.

Most cruises are out-and-back **7-day itineraries** through the Inside Passage into Southeast Alaska. Many lines sailing out of Seattle offer departures from Vancouver, BC. Cruise companies operate from Seattle's Bell Street (Pier 66) and Smith Cove (Pier 99) terminals. Alaska cruises sail to some combination of Tracey Arm Fjord, Juneau, Skagway, Ketchikan, Sitka and Glacier Bay; some head onward to Kodiak Island and Seward, the main gateway to the Alaska interior. Innumerable iterations may add in land-based journeys to the Yukon or Denali National Park or both. Most add a stop in Victoria, BC, usually on the homebound leg. Most ships carry 2,500 passengers;

but amenities onboard, like dining options and stateroom layouts, vary. Shore excursions range from a visit to a dogsledding camp and halibut fishing to flightseeing.

Cruise Lines

American Safari Cruises – 888-862-8881; www.innerseadiscoveries. com. 50-100 passenger boats.

Carnival – 800-764-7419; www. carnival.com. 7-day Alaska cruises.

Celebrity – 800-647-2251; www.celebritycruises.com. 7- to 12-day luxury cruises.

Holland America Line – 877-932-4259; www.hollandamerica.com. 7-day itineraries on mid-size ships.

Norwegian – 866-234-7350; www.ncl.com. 8-day itineraries start or end in Vancouver, BC.

Oceania – 800-531-5619; www.oceaniacruises.com. Mostly 7-day itineraries on luxury vessels with 600 passengers.

Princess – 800-774-6237; www.princess.com. Ships with moderate luxury.

Royal Caribbean – 866-562-7625; www.royalcaribbean.com. 7-day Alaska voyages on mid-size vessels (2,500 passengers).

Cruise ship at Seattle terminal

©Tim Thompson/Seattle's Convention and Visitors Bureau

PUGET SOUND

A 100mi-long inland sea, Puget Sound funnels through northwest Washington State, spilling around myriad islands and into bays, inlets and straits created by long-gone glaciers. The fingers of water extend south past the Seattle metropolitan region to the cities of Tacoma—a small city with a superlative cultural district—and Olympia, the state capital, where residents live quietly apart from the hubbub of the town's northern neighbors. To the north, the tidal waters flow past 35mi-long Whidbey Island and through the numerous islands and islets of the deservedly famous San Juan Islands, known for their pastoral landscapes and friendly residents. At the northern edge of the Puget Sound Basin, Bellingham is a low-key college town with easy access to outdoor recreation.

While wonders such as **orcas** still ply the waters, pollution and salmon-run declines threaten a natural system in which early settlers claimed one could walk across Elliott Bay on the backs of returning salmon. Until the Klondike gold rush brought worldwide attention and commerce, Seattle was not the preeminent city on Puget Sound; it was Tacoma. The two cities still observe a friendly rivalry, though Seattle is much larger. **Everett**, for its, part, has long had a military presence with the US navy. It's the home of the Boeing wide-body plant where 777s, 747s and 787s are assembled.

Coast Salish

The original inhabitants of Puget Sound, the Coast Salish, live on in their descendents and a couple of gorgeous new museums. The airy new (2012) **Suquamish Museum & Cultural Center** (www.suquamish. nsn.us), beyond Bainbridge Island, offers insights into the culture and origins of the Suquamish —the People of the Clear Salt Water — through sensory exhibits. Just east of Marysville, 34mi north of Seattle, the spectacular museum (2011) **Hibulb Cultural Center & Natural History Preserve** (www.hibulbculturalcenter.org) examines the history and culture of the Tulalip tribes; its entrance is adorned with exquisitely carved and decorated house poles.

Lime Kiln lighthouse, San Juan Island

©Robin Jacobson

Practical Information

When to Go

The months of May through mid-October are best for travel in the Puget Sound region, although the San Juan Islands—which are sunnier and drier than the rest of the region—are challenging to reach in July and August, since ferry lines are long. From mid-July through September, the entire region tends to be warm and dry, with summer temperatures averaging 75°F. Rain can be expected the rest of the year, with winter snowstorms common north of Everett.

Getting There and Around

♦ **By Air – Seattle-Tacoma International Airport** (SEA), also known as SEA-TAC (206-787-5388; www.portseattle.org), is the primary airport for Western Washington; the airport has rental-car agencies and connects to public transportation. **Kenmore Air** (425-486-1257; www.kenmoreair.com) provides daily flights to San Juan, Orcas and Lopez islands.

♦ **By Train – Amtrak** (800-USA-RAIL; www.amtrak.com) provides daily service to areas north and south of Seattle, stopping at Edmonds, Everett, Mount Vernon and Bellingham, as well as Tacoma, to the south. **SoundTransit** (888-889-6368; www.soundtransit.org) is a commuter rail service between Seattle, Everett and Tacoma.

♦ **By Ferry – Washington State Ferries** (206-464-6400; www.wsdot.com/ferries) provides daily car and foot-passenger transportation from Anacortes, 80mi north of Seattle, to the San Juan, Orcas, Lopez and Shaw islands in the San Juan Islands. During summer waits for ferries are lengthy, so it's best to get in line as early as possible, and plan for the extra wait time. Washington State Ferries also provides daily service to Whidbey Island, from Mukilteo (26mi north of Seattle) to Clinton, and from Port Townsend to Coupeville (the only route currently with a reservations option, highly recommended in summer). July through early September, **Clipper Vacations** runs a passenger-only vessel between Seattle and Friday Harbor, on San Juan Island; pre-season and post-season dates include whale-watching on this route.

♦ **By Bus – Greyhound** (800-231-2222; www.greyhound.com) serves communities throughout Puget Sound.

♦ **By Car** – The most convenient way to explore Puget Sound is by private vehicle; all major car-rental companies are represented at Sea-Tac International Airport.

Visitor Information

The **San Juan Islands Visitors Bureau** can be reached at 360-378-9551 or www.visitsanjuans.com. Additional Puget Sound region tourism bureaus include: **Tacoma** 253-627-2836, www.visit tacoma.com; **Bellingham** 360-671-3990, www.bellingham.org; **Olympia** 360-704-7544, www.visitolympia.com; **Skagit Valley**, www.visitskagitvalley.com; and **Whidbey Island**, www.whidbeycamanoislands.com.

⚓ SAN JUAN ISLANDS★★

This 172-island archipelago in the **Salish Sea** is the crown jewel of Washington State, attracting artists, craftspeople, writers and vacationers who come for bike riding, whale-watching, ⚓ **kayaking**, beachcombing and the tranquil pleasures of seaside living. The forest-cloaked islands are dotted with farmlands and small hamlets, and surrounded by sparkling waters. Only four of the islands—San Juan, Orcas, Lopez and Shaw—are reachable via public transit, aboard Washington State Ferries from the Anacortes terminal on the mainland; these routes are extremely popular in the summer, so extra wait time is advised.

The Whale Museum

©The Whale Museum

San Juan Island★★

See map p67. The most westerly of the three islands that offer visitor accommodations is also the most populous and the most diverse, with a **lavender farm**, vineyards, two lighthouses and two units of a National Historic Park. The main town, **Friday Harbor★** is the center of activity for all the islands. Art galleries, bookstores, boutiques and cafes cater to visitors as well as to its 8,000 residents.
The Whale Museum (*360-378-4710; www.whalemuseum.org*) introduces visitors to the resident

---

The Pig War

What would happen if they gave a war and nobody came? That's exactly what did happen on **San Juan Island** in 1859. That year, a long-running disagreement between Britain and the US over possession of the islands came to a head when a British settler shot an American homesteader's pig. Both countries sent large garrisons to the island and threatened war over the dispute; large military camps were established at opposite ends of the islands.

But no further shots were ever fired, and cooler heads in London and Washington, DC, decided to submit the issue to international arbitration. Meanwhile, soldiers on both sides drilled during the day—and spent evenings dancing, drinking, gambling and socializing together. The "war" came to an end in 1872 when Kaiser Wilhelm of Germany, who had been enlisted as the arbitrator, awarded the islands to the US. The two military camps now comprise the twin sections of **San Juan Islands National Historical Park★**, which is both explicitly and intrinsically dedicated to the cause of international peace.

65

pods of orcas and the ecosystem of the Salish Sea. You can sign up for whale and kayaking tours in Friday Harbor, or rent a bike or moped to explore more of the island.

One of the most scenic spots, **Roche Harbor★** was originally a Hudson's Bay Company camp; sitting above the harbor, historic Hotel de Haro overlooks a marina. Nearby, the **San Juan Islands Museum of Art Sculpture Park** features more than 100 sculptures, including kinetic works driven by breezes. The **San Juan Islands National Historical Park★**, with a section on each end of the island, commemorates the US and British encampments during the Pig War of 1859-1872, which ended with a peaceful resolution of ownership of the islands *(see sidebar previous page)*.

Orcas Island★★

This horseshoe-shaped island boasts the largest park and highest point in the islands, 5,252-acre **Moran State Park★**, where Mount Constitution rises 2,409ft, affording phenomenal views of the island-dotted sea; the park also has five lakes and miles of hiking trails. Eastsound is the island's hub, with shops, cafes and galleries, and a village green where the Saturday Farmers' Market is held. On the southeast edge of the island, **Doe Bay Resort & Retreat** is a rustic Northwest icon with cabins, clothing-optional soaking tubs and a cafe serving island-grown foods. **Deer Harbor**, on the opposite side of the island, offers whale and wildlife tours, and boat rentals.

Lopez Island★★

Lopez, where friendly waves from passing drivers is a local custom, is ideal for bike riding, with many miles of country lanes past farms and driftwood-jumbled beaches. **Spencer Spit State Park** has a long sand spit and a lagoon teeming with wildlife. **Lopez Village**, on Fisherman Bay, is the spot for buying groceries, enjoying a meal at a quaint cafe or sampling organic wine from Lopez Island Vineyards.

🐚 Whidbey Island

Just southeast of Lopez Island, Whidbey Island arcs in a narrow, 60mi curve through north Puget Sound. The island is a popular weekend getaway for Seattleites, who find appealing its bucolic tumble of hills, small towns, sand beaches and verdant farm fields interrupted only by a naval air station at the northern edge. The waterfront town of **Langley★**, on the southern end, is an iconic Northwest town, with charming wood-front buildings filled with shops, galleries and cafes. In spring, **gray whales** feed in the shallow waters off Langley. Beyond the town, **Greenbank Farm**, owned by the Nature Conservancy, has nature paths, art galleries, a wine shop, a cheese shop and a cafe known for Marionberry pies. Farther up-island, **Coupeville**, dating from the 1850s, harbors antiques shops and seafood restaurants, as well as Victorian houses built by 19C sea captains. The town is the locus of the sprawling, 27sq mi **Ebey's Landing National Historical Reserve★**, which protects the land and spirit of an entire rural community. Headquarters are in the **Island County Historical**

Museum (908 NW Alexander St.)
On the island's north end, the ruggedly spectacular **Deception Pass State Park★** is the site of the much-photographed **Deception Pass Bridge★**. It connects the two sides of Rosario Strait, beneath which turbulent tidal currents dash at up to 10mi/hr. The park features 6mi of saltwater shoreline with sand beaches and rocky cliffs, swimming lakes and wooded trails.

MOUNT BAKER AND THE NORTH CASCADES

The wild and craggy Cascade Mountains divide the wetter, western side of Washington from the drier eastern side. At the western edge of the **North Cascades,** just east of Bellingham, the volcanic sentinel of **Mount Baker** rises like a gigantic snow cone above the surrounding lowlands. South of Baker, the phenomenally scenic **North Cascades Highway** (see National Parks) ascends the Skagit River Valley through dense cedar and Douglas-fir forests to flower-filled alpine meadows along the Pacific Crest during spring, and blazing vine maples in fall.

North Cascades National Park★★

See National Parks Chapter.

Mount Baker

Near the Canadian border, Mount Baker juts skyward 10,778ft, its snowy prominence visible throughout much of Puget Sound. The mountain is best known for its wintertime scene, when it thrums with boarders and skiers, although its charms extend throughout the seasons. In spring visitors hike in search of avalanche lilies, huckleberries

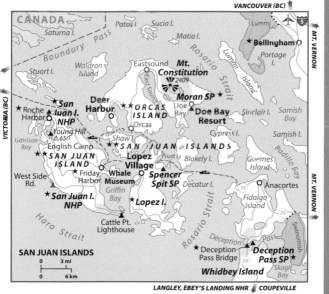

LANGLEY, EBEY'S LANDING NHR ◾ COUPEVILLE

PUGET SOUND

in the summer or fall colors in autumn. In winter the mountain is a powerhouse, with annual yields of 65ft or more of snow and steep, challenging terrain for hard-core ski enthusiasts.

En route, at Marblemount, the **Skagit River Bald Eagle Interpretive Center** (*www.skagiteagle.org*) offers information about these magnificent birds, which roost in riverside trees—as many as 200 at a time (*mid-Dec–Jan*). In Newhalem, the **North Cascades Visitor Center** (*206-386-4495; www.nps.gov*) features a video presentation and exhibits, as well as information about the park's campgrounds and 400mi of hiking trails, from short, scenic loops to strenuous climbs. Overlooks beyond Newhalem are well worth the stop; the turquoise waters of Ross and Diablo lakes glimmer in steep canyons at the foot of the towering Cascade peaks.

One of the best ways to experience the North Cascades is the **Seattle City Light Diablo Boat Tour** (*www.ncascades.org*), which begins at the 389ft Diablo Dam. A narrated lake cruise is followed by a Skagit Valley-sourced meal at the esteemed North Cascades Institute's lakeside Environmental Learning Center.

CITIES

BELLINGHAM★

North of Seattle 89mi and 20mi south of the Canadian border, the friendly college town of Bellingham (81,000) is known for its close proximity to the San Juan Islands and the ski slopes of Mount Baker, as well as Vancouver, British Columbia.

The city has a thriving cultural life, centered on the historic, Moorish-style 1927 **Mount Baker Theatre**, with its resident repertory theater company and symphony. A trio of small museums offer regional insights. The **Whatcom Museum★**, showcasing local history alongside art by regional artists, opened in the new Lightcatcher Building in 2009. A unique institution, the the **Spark Museum of Electrical Invention★★** (*360-738-3886; www.sparkmuseum.org*) presents artifacts related to electronics and broadcasting from 1580 through the 1950s. The **Bellingham Railway Museum** examines the history of railroads in Whatcom County. The **Fairhaven Historic District★** (*between 13th and 20th Sts.*) is a delightful mix of redbrick storefronts and restored Victorian houses inhabited by cafes, galleries and bookshops. Outdoor recreation is a big part of what makes Bellingham tick. **Whatcom Falls Park**, surrounding Whatcom Creek Gorge, features miles of ⛰ **hiking** trails past several waterfalls. To the south, 2,683-acre **Larrabee State Park** boasts 8,100sq ft of saltwater shoreline, plus two freshwater lakes for swimming and boating. The southern entrance to Bellingham, **Chuckanut Drive★**

(State Rte. 11) is an iconic Northwest scenic byway. The 21mi-long highway rounds tight curves, clinging to cliff sides overlooking the Salish Sea from the flatlands of Skagit Valley to Bellingham; several seafood restaurants line its route, offering cliffside dining with spectacular views.

OLYMPIA

The capital (pop. 47,000) of Washington State centers on the striking, white-domed 287ft **Capitol★** building. Completed in 1928, the neo-Classical building sports six massive bronze doors embossed with scenes symbolizing state history and industry, and a five-ton crystal Tiffany chandelier. Three blocks away, the **State Capitol Museum**, housed in a 1920s Italian Renaissance-style mansion, has exhibits that focus on the area's political and cultural history, as well as a lively program of activities, such as a Coast Salish button blanket craft workshop and classic movie screenings.

Despite the grandeur of the capitol building, Olympia has a small-town feel and a laidback vibe.

SKAGIT VALLEY

Drained by the westward-flowing Skagit River, this verdant valley is a fantasy of flower blooms in spring when thousands of acres of **tulips** and daffodils bloom in farm fields around Mount Vernon. One of the largest commercial bulb-cultivation regions in the world, the valley celebrates the spectacle every April during the **Skagit Valley Tulip Festival★★** (360-428-5959; www.tulipfestival.org).

The picturesque village of **La Conner★**, listed on the National Register of Historic Places, edges the Swinomish Channel off Skagit Bay. This artists' community boasts waterfront galleries, crafts shops, three museums and a charming ambiance that make it an attractive weekend destination for urbanites. The **Museum of Northwest Art★★** (121 S. First St.; 360-466-4446; www.museumofnwart.org) has a solid reputation for its works by Northwest master artists, including Guy Anderson and Morris Graves. Nearby, the **La Conner Quilt & Textile Museum** is a slice of Americana, with a permanent collection that dates to 1820, and traveling exhibits.

TACOMA

Situated on deep-water **Commencement Bay** 32mi southwest of Seattle, Tacoma boasts the largest international shipping port in the state. The city has reinvented itself from a 19C port and timber town that suffered considerable decline into a modern city of 200,000 with an active museum district. Near the Tacoma Dome sports stadium, the new LeMay car museum (see Museums) opened in 2012.

The star of the city's bustling Theater District is the ornate, 1918 **Pantages Theater**, modeled after the theater in the Palace of Versailles. Additional theaters include the 1918 Beaux Arts-style **Rialto** and the intimate, contemporary **Theatre on the Square**. All three theaters are run by the Broadway Center for the Performing Arts, which serves as home to arts groups ranging from the Tacoma Symphony Orchestra to the Tacoma Opera.

MUSEUMS

PUGET SOUND

Fort Nisqually Living History Museum★★

Point Defiance Park, Tacoma. 253-591-5339. www.fortnisqually.org. Open summer daily 11am–5pm. Winter Wed–Sun 11am–4pm. $6.50.

The park is a restoration of the first Hudson's Bay Company **trading post** on Puget Sound. Two original buildings are surrounded by a blacksmith shop, demonstration kitchen, re-created dry goods store and other shops. Re-enactors demonstrate butter churning and wagon wheel building.

LeMay—America's Car Museum★★

2702 East D. St. 253-779-8490. www.lemaymuseum.org. Open summer daily 10am–5pm. Winter Wed–Sun 10am–5pm. $14.

This four-story museum with sleek architectural lines and high spruce ceilings displays 350 vehicles at a time from a much larger collection. Exhibits range from horseless carriages to sleek DeLoreans with gull wing doors. Other attractions include a kids' activities area, driving simulators, a cafe, a theater, a field for car shows, concerts and even drive-in movies.

Museum of Glass★★

1801 Dock St., Tacoma. 866-468-7386. www.museumofglass.org. Open year-round daily 10am–5pm (noon Sun in summer); closed Mon–Tue in winter. $12.

This museum (2002), designed by Arthur Erickson, reflects the fact that Tacoma is known for its glass art, thanks to internationally famous son **Dale Chihuly**. Its 90ft-tall stainless-steel cone rises above the industrial Thea Foss Waterway; inside are a glassblowing facility, geared toward audiences, and galleries filled with traveling displays. The 500-ft-long **Chihuly Bridge of Glass** connects the museum's rooftop plaza with the restored Union Station.

Tacoma Art Museum★★

1701 Pacific Ave., Tacoma. 253-272-4258. www.tacomaart museum.org. Open Wed–Sun 10am–5pm (til 8pm Thu). $10, third Thu free 5pm–8pm.

This design by Antoine Predock (2003) houses **Northwest art** of Jacob Lawrence, Morris Graves and others. Northwest **glass art**, with emphasis on Chihuly's works is a central focus of TAM. The museum will double in size in 2014 when a new wing opens for a Western American art collection. On the top floor, spaces allow guests to create their own works of art.

Washington State History Museum★★

1911 Pacific Ave. Open daily, 10am–5pm summer; Wed–Sun 10am–5pm winter. $9.50. 888-238-4373. www.wshs.org.

In nine thematic exhibit areas, life-size **dioramas** and voice-overs dramatize the growth of the state, from European-Indian encounters to modern challenges. All are presented through interactive means.

MUST SEE

THE GREAT OUTDOORS

Point Defiance Park★

5400 N. Pearl St., Tacoma. 253-305-1000. www.metroparkstacoma.org. Open daily half hour before dawn–half hour after dusk.

At 702 acres, Point Defiance Park is one of the largest city parks in the nation. It has plenty of places to enjoy the out-of-doors, whether hiking through the park's dense stands of old-growth Douglas-fir forest; watching bald eagles dive for salmon in the tidal rapids below 250ft cliffs; beachcombing at **Owen's Beach** or strolling through the rose, dahlia or Japanese gardens. The **Point Defiance Zoo and Aquarium★** sits near the park's entrance, and the **Fort Nisqually Living History Museum★★** is located on a 5mi forested loop drive that offers viewing opportunities of raccoons as they scamper along the road shoulder, and the Tacoma Narrows Bridge and waterway. Outside the park's entrance is a Washington State Ferries dock for ferries bound for nearby, rural **Vashon Island**.

Point Defiance Zoo & Aquarium★

5400 N Pearl St., Tacoma. 253-591-5337. www.pdza.org. Open summer daily 8:30am–6pm. Rest of the year hours vary. $16.

More than 350 species of animals can be found at this compact, 19-acre zoo and aquarium. The zoo's successful breeding program for the endangered red wolf has resulted in wolves being re-introduced to their natural habitats. The exhibit **Red Wolf Woods** is among the best, with close-up views of these magnificent animals.
The South Pacific aquarium's massive **lagoon** is filled with brilliantly colored tropical fish, while the **North Pacific tank** is home to salmon, giant Pacific octopus and more.
Recent additions to the zoo include (2011) **Cats of the Canopy**, with clouded leopards, **Asian Forest Sanctuary** with rare Sumatran tigers, and an outdoor animal theater.

©Point Defiance Zoo & Aquarium

Point Defiance Zoo & Aquarium

71

EXCURSIONS

Nisqually National Wildlife Refuge★

101 Brown Farm Rd., 10mi east of Olympia via I-5, Exit 114, then half-mile on Brown Farm Rd. 360-753-9467. www.fws.gov/Nisqually. Open year-round dawn–dusk.

In 2009, the Northwest's largest tidal marsh restoration project removed 5mi of dikes, allowing saltwater to return to 732 acres of the Nisqually River Delta. The project reintroduced nutrient-rich habitat for Puget Sound salmon and a host of avian species, including many migratory birds. Boardwalks permit grand views.

Wolf Haven International

111 Offut Lake Rd SE, Tenino, 11 mi south of Olympia. 360-264-4695. www.wolfhaven.org. Open Apr–Sept Wed–Sat 10am–4pm, Sun noon–4pm. Rest of the year Sat 10am–4pm, Sun noon–4pm. $12.

This wildlife rehabilitation center and sanctuary houses primarily

Orcas

The orca, or killer whale, the largest member of the dolphin family, is well-known for close family ties and a complex culture, including a dialect unique to each pod. Seattle is the world's only major metropolitan area with a **resident population** of orcas. Three pods—J, K and L—forage for salmon in Sound waters, each matriarchal family led by an older female. These leviathans are easy to spot from Washington State ferries; look for sleek dorsal fins breaking the water.

captive-raised wolves—more than three dozen animals, including US wolves, Mexican gray wolves, red wolves and wolf-dog mixes. Docents lead guided tours to educate the public about this species. The most unusual aspect of this preserve is the popular monthly **Howl-In** in summer, when families are invited to an evening's entertainment that includes howling with the wolves.

Wolf Haven International

©Julie Lawrence for Wolf Haven International

OLYMPIC PENINSULA

The thumb of Washington state, Olympic Peninsula is the westernmost point of the continental US, extending from Puget Sound west to the Pacific Ocean. The Strait of Juan de Fuca forms its northern boundary, Route 12 its southern border, and Hood Canal, an 80mi-long inlet of Puget Sound, divides it from the mainland to the east. To the north are the small towns of Port Angeles and Sequim, and at its northeast edge, the Victorian seaport of Port Townsend. One of the most scenic places in the country, the peninsula claims diverse landscapes and climatic variations that make it one of the driest places on the continent (less than 15 inches of rain a year) as well as one of the wettest (with record annual rainfall of 190 inches). Vast Olympic National Park dominates its north-central interior; its centerpiece, the Olympic Mountain Range, includes ice-bound Mount Olympus sitting at 7,965ft and flanked by rain-forested valleys that meet wild Pacific Ocean beaches.

CITIES

PORT TOWNSEND★★

Occupying the northeast tip of the Olympic Peninsula, at the mouth of Puget Sound, the town exudes a distinct maritime charm. This beloved Northwest destination is one of the best preserved examples of a **Victorian seaport** in the US. Its historic district is a UNESCO World Heritage Site; Victorian-era brick and stone buildings on the waterfront house art galleries, shops and cafes. A historic fort at the edge of town is fronted by a broad sweep of golden sand.

Before settlers arrived, the **S'Klallam Indians** used Admiralty Inlet as canoe portage to bypass treacherous currents at the peninsula's tip. Capt. **George Vancouver** named the sheltered harbor he saw in 1792 Port Townsend. The town was founded in 1851; three years later, the US government transferred its customs district headquarters here, a move that made the town an important center for maritime trade.

©Port Townsend Marine Science Center

Learning from Orcas exhibit, Port Townsend Marine Science Center

Practical Information

When to Go

The weather is much more reliable in summer (July and August are the driest months) and fall on the peninsula. The region is slow to warm up in the spring, and with the exception of the Sequim area, rainfall is frequent October through June. (Rain in the rain forests can be expected nearly year-round.) However, the region's highways are crowded in summer, especially on weekends.

Getting There and Getting Around

♦ **By Air** – **Kenmore Air Express** (425-486-1257; www.kenmoreair. com) offers daily service between Seattle-Tacoma International Airport and the Port Angeles' Fairchild Intl Airport.

♦ **By Ferry** – To reach the Olympic Peninsula via **Washington State Ferries** (206-464-6400; www.wsdot.com/ferries) from downtown Seattle, take the Bainbridge Island ferry, or from north Seattle, take the Edmonds to Kingston ferry. There is also a ferry from Coupeville, on Whidbey Island, to Port Townsend (you can make advance reservations for this ferry).

♦ **By Bus** – **Olympic Bus Lines** (360-417-0700; www.olympic buslines.com) provides twice daily service between Seattle locales, including Seattle-Tacoma International Airport, Seattle Greyhound and Seattle Amtrak, and Port Angeles, Sequim and Port Townsend on Olympic Peninsula.

♦ **By Car** – The only way to see the vast majority of peninsula sights is by car. From Seattle, there are three ways to reach the peninsula: crossing Puget Sound aboard a Washington State Ferry; crossing the Tacoma Narrows Bridge and then crossing the Hood Canal Bridge; or (the slower, scenic route), driving through Olympia and around Hood Canal.

Visitor Information

The **Olympic Peninsula Visitor Bureau**: 360-452-8552; www.olympicpeninsula.org. **Olympic National Park Main Visitor Center** (360-565-3131; www.nps.gov/olym) is located at 3002 Mt. Angeles Road in Port Angeles, just south of US 101, on the road to Hurricane Ridge; it provides free maps and information about the park.

Accommodations

There are four lodges in Olympic National Park as well as park campgrounds. Access www.olympicnationalparks.com for information and reservations. Peripheral towns also offer various types of lodging and dining.

Today several museums offer insights into the town's past, including **Rothschild House Historic Museum** (*Taylor and Franklin sts.*) and **Jefferson County Historical Museum** (*see p76*).

At the new **Northwest Maritime Center** (*431 Water St.*), visitors can converse with boat builders as they replicate historic small craft. Just north of downtown, **Fort Worden State Park★★** (*360-*

Historic Port Gamble

Victorian charm abounds at a historic hamlet on a bend of State Route 104, just west of the Hood Canal Bridge. The community of **Port Gamble★**, a National Historic Landmark that was once a company sawmill town, looks like a movie set, with tidy, New England-style homes (some of them antiques shops) set behind white picket fences, and a wooden church crowned by a tall steeple. The **Port Gamble General Store & Café** features a shell museum, old-time candy shop and cafe.

Northwest Maritime Center

©Miller Full

344 4400; www.parks.wa.gov/fortworden) preserves 200 officers' homes, barracks, bunkers and the **Commanding Officer's Quarters Museum** on a greensward lined with grand old trees. Below lies a crescent beach lapped by calm waves in summer. The water is too cold for swimming, but a kayak rental shop at the beach does a booming business. A nearby pier holds the town's **Marine Science Center** (532 Battery Way; 360-385-5582; www.ptmsc.org), with touch tanks and displays; its **hydrophone** picks up vocalizations of passing whales. **Point Wilson Lighthouse**, at the far end of the beach, is backed by the snowy heights of Mount Baker in the distance.

SEQUIM

With annual rainfall of just 15 inches, Sequim (pronounced Skwim) and its 6,000 residents sit in the center of Washington's "banana belt," drawing sun-worshipping retirees and tourists. The **Museum and Arts Center in the Sequim-Dungeness Valley** (175 W. Cedar St.) explores topics ranging from the nearby Jamestown S'Klallam Tribe to a much-studied mastodon rib bone excavated in 1977 with a spear point embedded in it.

West of town, the 32mi-long **Dungeness River** flows north to the Strait of Juan de Fuca. The Dungeness Valley is home to more than 30 **lavender farms★**, many of them extending the welcome mat to visitors. In July rolling waves of dusky lavender extend to the horizon, and farm shops proffer fragrant emollients and gifts.

Martha Lane Lavender

Courtesy of the Sequim Lavender Growers Association

Sequim's **Lavender Weekend** (*www.lavenderfestival.com*) brings farm tours and a street fair; many of the farms are also open for self-guided tours.

PORT ANGELES

Tucked between the Olympic Mountains and the Strait of Juan de Fuca—the waterbody that separates the Olympic Peninsula from Vancouver Island—Port Angeles is the county seat, a commercial center and a pass-through for visitors en route to Victoria, BC, via the Coho Ferry, or Olympic National Park. One of the major access routes into the heart of the park, Hurricane Ridge Road, begins inside city limits.

The town is situated at the edge of a deep harbor, protected by the 2.5mi-long Ediz Hook, with a Coast Guard station and lighthouse positioned at the tip. The **Arthur D. Fiero Marine Life Center** (*315 N. Lincoln St.*), on the city pier, is a compact marine education center staffed by volunteers.

Some 2,700 years ago, the town's waterfront was the setting for the Native American village of Tse-whit-zen, which saw the light of day again during an excavation in 2003. Some 67,000 artifacts have been recovered to date. This history and that of succeeding waves of settlers is explained in the **Museum at the Carnegie** (*207 S. Lincoln St.*). High on a hill overlooking the bay, the **Port Angeles Fine Arts Center** (*1203 E. Lauridsen Blvd.*) and adjacent Webster Woods feature works by local artists displayed in indoor and outdoor settings.

MUSEUMS

Jefferson County Historical Museum

540 Water St., Port Townsend. 360-385-1003. www.jchsmuseum.org. Open year-round daily 11am–4pm. $4.

Housed inside the handsome red-brick 1892 **City Hall**, this small museum is a repository of local memories, with exhibits on the Victorian era and the region's rowdy maritime era, as well as regional military history and the town's (now long-gone) Chinatown. Also on display are baskets, carvings and other artifacts from peninsula tribes.

Museum at the Carnegie

207 S. Lincoln St., Port Angeles. 360-452-2662. www.clallam historicalsociety.com. Open year-round Wed–Sat 1pm–4pm. $2.

A 1919 Carnegie library is the setting for this regional museum, whose main exhibit, **Strong People: Faces of Clallam County**, introduces the settlers—loggers, fishermen and farmers—who helped build the community. Visitors can also hear three local tribal languages in **Our Ancestral Heritage**, and learn what forces created the topography in Olympic National Park.

THE GREAT OUTDOORS

Olympic National Park★★★ *See National Parks chapter.*

Dungeness National Wildlife Reserve★

15mi east of Port Angeles on Kitchen-Dick Rd. off Hwy 101. 360-683-5847. www.fws.gov. Open year-round daily dusk–dawn. $3.

An 1857 lighthouse (occasionally open for tours) tops a narrow, 5mi-long finger of sand, one of the world's longest natural spits. The serene bay and eelgrass-laden tidal flats here harbor seals, bald eagles and migrating shorebirds.

Olympic Discovery Trail★

Access trail in Railroad Bridge Park, W. Hendrickson Rd., Sequim. www.olympicdiscoverytrail.com.

Edging farmlands and the Strait of Juan de Fuca, a 20mi segment, from Sequim west to Port Angeles, of the proposed paved 130mi **recreational trail** is complete,

Salt Creek Recreation Area

©Olympic Peninsula Visitor Bureau

as is a 30mi mountain-biking segment west of Port Angeles that continues to Lake Crescent. Bike rental shops are available in Sequim and Port Angeles.

Salt Creek Rec. Area

15mi west of Port Angeles on Camp Hayden Rd. 360-928-3441. www.clallam.net/countyparks.

A 196-acre park with sand beach and uplands, this area offers rewarding tide-pooling. Crevices in the rocks at the **Tongue Point Marine Sanctuary** hold myriad sea creatures and mussels.

Dungeness Spit, Dungeness National Wildlife Reserve

©Russ Veenema

EXCURSIONS

Makah Cultural and Research Center★★

The center is on Bayview Ave. in Neah Bay (see below). 360-645-2711. www.makah.com. Open year-round daily 10am–5pm. $5.

Research indicates that the Makah have inhabited this coastal region at the northwestern tip of the Olympic Peninsula for at least 4,000 years. This world-class museum showcases archaeological artifacts from the ancient Ozette Village, "America's Pompeii," which was buried by a mudslide 500 years ago. More than 55,000 priceless artifacts form the core of the collection. A Makah **longhouse** and seagoing cedar canoes here help celebrate the history of the Makah Nation.

Neah Bay

From Hwy. 101, take Hwy. 112 to Clallam Bay and turn northwest for Neah Bay, in the Makah Indian Reservation.

Neah Bay is the only town on the Makah Indian Reservation. Its chief attraction is the cultural center (see above). West of Neah Bay, the **Cape Flattery Trail** is a .75-mile boardwalk to a forested headland where viewing platforms afford spectacular views of the Pacific Ocean—gray and humpback whales are often spotted—and forbidden **Tatoosh Island**, a sacred place for the Makah Nation. South of town lies magical **Shi Shi Beach★★**, with sea-stack sentinels, tide pools and a broad sweep of pristine sand. For directions to the trailhead and a recreational pass,

stop by **Washburn's General Store** (*1450 Bayview Ave.*) in Neah Bay. Farther south, the **Lake Ozette Trail** is a popular 9mi loop of boardwalks that leads to sand beaches and rocky headlands.

Hood Canal

30mi southeast of Sequim via Hwy. 101 to Quilcene, then about 28mi to intersection with Hwy. 106. To drive both sides of the canal, head east on Hwy. 101 and continue north on Hwy. 3.

Driving around Hood Canal, a saltwater fjord on the west side of Puget Sound, makes a scenic excursion that incorporates spectacular beaches and slow-paced hamlets. Highways 101 and 106 traverse the byways of the canal on the east side of the Olympic Peninsula and the west side of the Kitsap Peninsula. These routes feature some of the state's most idyllic beaches, including **Potlatch State Park** (Hwy. 101), with more than a mile of saltwater shoreline; **Twanoh State Park** (off Hwy. 106), with the warmest saltwater swimming area in the state; and **Belfair State Park** (*Hwy. 106*), with tidal flats and a saltwater swimming area. Hood Canal is renowned for shellfish; the **Hama Hama Seafood Store** in Lilliwaup sells the famed Hamma Hamma oysters, which have a clean, crisp flavor and firm meat. To get out on the water, you can rent kayaks at Pleasant Harbor, a few miles south of Brinnon.

SOUTHWEST WASHINGTON

Southwest Washington is a diverse terrain, with the towering peaks of the Cascade Range, oak prairies and Douglas-fir forests, sandy Pacific Ocean beaches and marine life-filled bays. In the interior, the highest peak of the Cascade Range, volcanic Mount Rainier (14,410ft) offers world-class hiking and sightseeing, while volcanic Mount St. Helens (8,363ft) lends fascinating insights into nature's forces and self-healing ability. Long before George Vancouver sailed into Puget Sound in 1792, Native Americans knew the now-famous peaks well. Hunting only on the lower slopes, they realized the "smoking" mountains held danger. Mid-19C settlers, however, attempted to climb Rainier, and in the 20C developed resorts in the area. Scientists believe that Rainier is stable even though St. Helens has blown her top. Meanwhile on the coast, family fun and historic sites await visitors on Long Beach Peninsula, and a historic fort adds interest to the Columbia River recreational haven of Vancouver (in Washington, of course, not Canada).

MOUNT ST. HELENS NATIONAL VOLCANIC MONUMENT★★★

Open year-round daily. Visitor center at 3029 Spirit Lake Hwy., Toutle; 360-274-0962; www.parks.wa.gov/stewardship/mountsthelens; open May–mid-Sept daily 9am–5pm, rest of the year 4pm; closed major holidays. 360-449-7800. www.fs.usda.gov/mountsthelens. $5.

One of the world's most famous volcanoes, Mount St. Helens erupted in 1980 with the intensity of 500 atomic bombs, destroying its northern flank and blasting away more than 1,300ft of elevation. In 1982 the US Congress declared Mount St. Helens a National Volcanic Monument. Today the eviscerated mountain, surrounded by a 172sq-mi preserve, is a leading visitor attraction.

Mount St. Helens National Volcanic Monument

©MountStHelens.com

Practical Information

When to Go

July is the best time to see flower-filled alpine meadows at Mt. Rainier, but any summer day through September offers the best opportunity for clear weather and great views at both Rainier and Mount St. Helens. Summertime frequently brings fog to the Washington coast, so the best times to visit are the shoulder seasons or winter-storm season.

Getting There and Getting Around

♦ **By Air** – **Sea-Tac International Airport** (SEA) (206-787-5388; www.portseattle.org) is the primary air hub for travelers to Mt. Rainier; **Portland International Airport** (PDX) (503-460-4040; www.flypdx.com) is the closest air hub to Mount St. Helens, Vancouver, WA, and the Long Beach Peninsula.

♦ **By Train** – **Amtrak** (800-USA-RAIL; www.amtrak.com) provides daily service from Seattle and Portland to Vancouver, WA.

♦ **By Bus** – **Greyhound** (214-849-8966; www.greyhound.com) provides regularly scheduled bus service from Seattle and Portland to select communities throughout Western Washington.

Pacific Transit System (360-875-9418; www.pacifictransit.org) serves Long Beach communities and other Southwest Washington destinations.

♦ **By Car** – Southwest Washington is easiest to visit by car; Sea-Tac and Portland airports both have all the major car-rental agencies.

Visitor Information

Mount Rainier NP Headquarters (360-569-2211; www.nps.gov/mora).
Mount St. Helens NVM (360-449-7800; www.fs.usda.gov/mountsthelens).
Long Beach Peninsula Visitors Bureau (360-642-2400; www.funbeach.com).
Vancouver Tourism (360-750-1553; www.visitvancouverusa.com).

Accommodations

Paradise Inn and **National Park Inn** provide overnight lodging within Mt. Rainier National Park; for rates and reservations: 360-569-2400 www.mtrainierguest services.com. The park has four campgrounds; for fees and reservations: www.nps.gov/mora. Area towns offer a number of lodging options.
There are no accommodations in Mt. St. Helens National Volcanic Monument.

Youngest of the major Cascade volcanoes, St. Helens was known to ancient Native Americans as "Fire Mountain." Quiet through most of the 20C, the conical mountain rumbled slowly awake in the spring of 1980, for several weeks giving off warning quakes and hisses.

The sudden explosion on May 18 blasted a column of ash 15mi into the air and turned day to night as it drifted eastward; it poured hot rock and pumice over the countryside, felled 250sq mi of forest, caused severe flooding and left 57 people dead. When the eruption was over, the 9,677ft peak measured only 8,363ft. Its crater measured 2,000ft deep and about 1mi wide.

Mount St. Helens Visitor Center at Silver Lake★★

Rte. 504, 5mi east of I-5, Castle Rock Exit (see address and hours p79).

This center makes a good starting point for a visit. Inside you can view a fascinating live-footage film, a slide show and worthwhile exhibits. From here, Spirit Memorial Highway (504) leads to the **Johnston Ridge Observatory**.

Johnston Ridge Observatory★★★

At end of Hwy. 504, Toutle, 360-274-2140. www.fs.usda. gov/mountsthelens. 52mi east of I-5. Open mid-May–Oct daily 10am–6pm. $8.

This visitor center sits within 5mi of the volcano's crater, offering fine **views★★★** of the devastation, still vividly apparent, though regenerated forest is making a strong appearance. Be sure to view the 16min **film** about the 1980 eruption in the 280 seat theater.

MOUNT RAINIER NATIONAL PARK★★★

See National Parks chapter.

LONG BEACH PENINSULA★★

Stretching 28mi from the Columbia River to the mouth of **Willapa Bay**, this peninsula is a spectacular land of sand dunes and small, friendly communities, Pacific Ocean-pounded beaches on one side and the placid bay on the other. Originally inhabited by **Chinook Indians**, the area is famous as the site where Lewis and Clark reached the shores of the Pacific in 1805. The **Lewis and Clark Interpretive Center★** in **Cape Disappointment State Park** (*360-642-3029; www.parks wa.gov*) outlines their journey of exploration and provides a view of the ironically named **Cape Disappointment**, where the explorers had their first, awe-inspiring look at the tumultuous Pacific. The park, with **trails** winding through dense salal bushes along blufftops and down to wave-washed coves, is home to two historic lighthouses.
The peninsula is famed as a

Cape Disappointment State Park

SOUTHWEST WASHINGTON

Lewis and Clark Interpretive Center

©Washington State Parks and Recreation

draw visitors, and local eateries feature **Willapa Bay oysters**, famed for their quality.

VANCOUVER

This Washington State city (pop. 166,000) lies on the north bank of the **Columbia River** northwest of Portland. Vancouver is the setting for the reconstructed **Fort Vancouver National Historic Site** *(see opposite)*. Situated between Mount St. Helens (north), the Cascade Range (east) and the Columbia River Gorge (south), the city has more than 7,000 acres of parks. Stately Victorian houses along **Officers Row** include the Queen Anne Victorian **George C. Marshall House** *(no. 1301; open for tours)* and the 1849 **Grant House** *(no. 1101)*, now a restaurant. The **Pearson Air Museum** *(at* Pearson Field; 360-694-7026; www. pearsonairmuseum.org) showcases WWI and WWII aircraft.

summertime family destination, with kite flying on its beaches, bike riding along the 8.2mi **Discovery Trail** and hiking through pinewoods at **Leadbetter Point State Park**, home of the threatened Western **snowy plover**, which lay their nests in the sand dunes here.

The small but lively **World Kite Museum** *(see below)* and the rustic **Cranberry Museum** (360-642-5553; www.cranberrymuseum.com)

MUSEUM

🏔 World Kite Museum★

303 Sid Snyder Dr., Long Beach. 360-642-4020. kitefestival.com. Open May–Sept daily 11am–5pm. Rest of the year Fri–Tue. $5.

A kaleidoscope of colors greets visitors to the World Kite Museum, where everything from Asian fighting kites to decorative kites from around the world are on display. On the third week of August annually this small, lively museum sponsors the **Washington State International Kite Festival**, which fills the sky with legions of unique kites and draws thousands of spectators.

International Kite Festival

©Bill Rogers/World Kite Museum

HISTORICAL SITE

Fort Vancouver National Historic Site★★★

612 E. Reserve St., Vancouver. 360-816-6230. www.nps.gov/fova. Open year-round Mon–Sat 9am–5pm, Sun noon–5pm (visitor center 10am–5pm). $3.

Situated in the city limits, Fort Vancouver was the historic Columbia headquarters and chief supply depot of the British fur-trading **Hudson's Bay Company** from 1825 to 1860. Ironically it fostered American settlement of the Pacific Northwest. A US army post was subsequently installed at the site. The fort was expanded and designated a National Historic Site in 1961. Archaeological findings here have been important for valid interpretation of the site. Visitors can stroll through an accurate re-creation of the fort, complete with reconstructed buildings that include a carpenter shop, a bakery, a fur-storage building and a blacksmith shop. Re-enactors bring the past to life at regularly scheduled events.

Fort Vancouver National Historic Site

Courtesy National Park Service

Preserving an Estuary
The **Willapa National Wildlife Refuge**, on 260sq-mi Willapa Bay—the second-largest estuary on the West Coast—shelters several important ecosystems, from salt marshes and muddy tideflats to coastal dunes and beaches. Numerous types of fish and shellfish spawn here; the bay provides habitat for more than 100,000 shorebirds annually during spring migration; and its isolated sandbars provide pupping grounds for **harbor seals**. In recent years invasive species have invaded the bay; efforts are underway to contain their spread.

Fort Vancouver National Historic Site, Campfires and Candlelight Tour

©Brian Christopher of Christopher Communications

SOUTHWEST WASHINGTON

83

EXCURSIONS

Northwest Trek Wildlife Park★★

6mi north of Eatonville, on Rte. 161. 360-832-6117; www.nwtrek.org. Open Jul-Aug daily 9:30am-6pm; Rest of the year hours vary. $17.

This 725-acre zoological park displays animals native to the Pacific Northwest. On **walking tours** and **tram rides**, visitors are treated to close views of bison, elk, big-horn sheep and other large mammals. In the hands-on **discovery center**, toads, snakes and salamanders are the focus of attention. Nature **trails** and a new **zip-line** and agility course add fun.

Northwest Trek Wildlife Park

©Northwest Trek Wildlife Park

Crystal Mountain Resort★

33914 Crystal Mountain Blvd., off Hwy. 410. 360.663.2265. www.crystalmountainresort.com.

Located northeast of the national park, this 2,600-acre resort is the largest ski operation in the state, with 50 ski runs, 11 chair lifts and a new, high-speed gondola that whisks visitors to a 6,872ft summit. In summer the gondola offers speedy access to scenic alpine hiking.

Lewis and Clark Interpretive Center★

4mi south of Long Beach, at 248 Robert Gray Dr., in Ilwaco. 360-642-3029. www.parks.wa.gov. Open Mar–Nov daily 10am–5pm. Rest of the year Wed–Sun. $5.

On a high bluff where Pacific waves meet the Columbia River, this interpretive center is an excellent small museum that illuminates the epic 1905 arrival of the explorers at the Pacific. Exhibits include timeline wall panels, paintings, photographs, a short film and journal quotes. Visitors can watch the dramatic wave action below—and migrating gray whales in January and March—from a glassed-in observation deck.

Northwest Carriage Museum★

47mi northeast of Long Beach, at 314 Alder St., in Raymond. 360-942-4150. www.nwcarriage museum.org. Open May–Sept Wed–Sat 10am–4pm, Sun-Tue noon–4pm. Rest of the year closed Wed–Sun. $4.

The compact, but well executed museum features finely restored 19C vehicles—carriages, buggies and the like—including a horse-drawn carriage used in the movie *Gone with the Wind*.

EASTERN WASHINGTON

Open, dry and rugged, the vast expanse of eastern Washington stretches from the foothills of the Cascades to the Idaho border, and from Walla Walla north to the Okanogan highlands. It is largely lumped under the geographic term the Columbia Basin. Rivers cut deep, meandering canyons across the arid land, punctuated by fragrant pine forests and Irrigated orchards near the Cascades. Hydroelectric power from dams like the Grand Coulee brought irrigation water to thousands of acres, and the region now is a major producer of fresh fruit, potatoes, wheat, vegetables and wine. The East's abundant sunshine—averaging more than 100 sunny days annually—makes it ideal for wine production: Numerous vineyards in 13 viticultural areas grow grapes for world-class wines and offer tours. Visitors who explore this region will find appealing natural areas, parks, museums and historic sites as well.

CITIES

WINTHROP★

Lying less than 50mi due south of the Canadian border, in the Methow Valley, this Old West-style town is a quintessential stop for those driving the famed Cascade Loop. Its wooden sidewalks and false-fronted buildings appeal to visitors, yet original buildings from the late 18C mining boom include pioneer log cabins, a print shop, saloons and hotels. The ice cream is homemade at **Sheri's Sweet Shoppe**, and the Rocking Horse Bakery uses locally grown grains in their baked goods.

Winthrop is a hub of outdoor recreation, whether swimming at nearby **Lake Pearrygin**, floating down the Methow River, biking on an extensive trail network or cross-country skiing on more than 100mi of cross-country ski trails.

Leavenworth

©Leavenworth Channel

Practical Information

When to Go

Late spring and early fall are the best times to visit. In spring orchards are in bloom and it's sunny and mild. In late summer and fall, peaches, pears and apples are for sale at roadside stands and the temperature is more comfortable. The average daily temperature in July and August is 82°F, yet 90°F days are common.

Getting There and Around

♦ **By Air** – **Spokane International Airport** (509-455-6429; www.spokaneairports.net) is the area's main air travel hub.
♦ **By Bus** – Greyhound (214-849-8966; www.greyhound.com) provides regularly scheduled bus service to communities throughout Eastern Washington.
♦ **By Car** – Distances are vast in Eastern Washington, and the only reasonable way to see the region's top attractions is by private car. All of the major car-rental agencies can be found at Spokane International Airport.

Visitor Information

Spokane (509-624-1341, www.visitspokane.com); **Leavenworth** (509-548-5807, www.leavenworth.org); **Walla Walla** (509-529-4718, www.wallawalla.org); **Wenatchee** (509-886-5113, www.wenatcheevalley.org), **Winthrop** (509-996-2125, www.winthropwashington.com) and **Yakima** (509-575-3010, www.visityakima.com).

LEAVENWORTH★★

This Cascade Range town, tucked into a mountain valley, sports Bavarian-style architecture (even in its banks and grocery stores), alpine murals and flower baskets brimming with blooms in summer. Store clerks are garbed in traditional dirndls, oompah music plays everywhere and a bratwurst stand does a brisk business. Boutiques on tidy streets sell local chocolates, nutcrackers and old-time wooden toys.

At the town's center, a gazebo features live music during **Art in the Park** (*May-Oct*). Leavenworth's biggest celebrations are the **Autumn Leaf Festival** (*Sept*), **Oktoberfest** and the **Christmas Lighting Festival**.

Nearby recreation includes hikes in the Alpine Lakes Wilderness, rafting down the **Wenatchee River**, golf and Nordic skiing.

WENATCHEE

Surrounded by orchards, Wenatchee is tucked into a valley at the confluence of the Wenatchee and Columbia rivers. Washington State is the nation's leading producer of 🍎 **apples**, and Wenatchee is the "Apple Capital of Washington."

The **Washington Apple Commission Visitor Center** (*2900 Euclid Ave.; 509-663-9600; www.bestapples.com*) has a compact exhibit. The **Wenatchee Valley Museum and Cultural Center** (*127 S. Mission; 509-888-6240; www.wenatcheevalley.org*) has a historical exhibit on apple production as well as displays on the Native people of the Columbia Plateau and the mystery of the 11,000-year-old Clovis people (a Clovis site was discovered in Wenatchee in 1987).

The paved **Apple Valley Recreation Loop Trail** traverses both sides of the Columbia River, crossing bridges on the north and south ends of town and looping through several riverfront parks. Nearby, **Ohme Gardens** (www.ohmegardens.com) is a reproduction of alpine environments.

SPOKANE★

Near the Idaho border, Washington's second largest city (210,000 residents) spreads along the wooded slopes of the Spokane River. Its downtown holds dozens of historic buildings along a stretch of river where waterfalls plummet over basalt lava cliffs. **Riverfront Park★★** offers rolling lawns shaded by ponderosa pines, landscaped walkways, a restored 1909 **carousel★**, the **SkyRide★** gondola that descends 200ft to the base of Lower Spokane Falls, a small amusement park and an IMAX theater. A major arts center, the city hosts the Spokane Symphony at the ornate Art Deco-style **Fox**. The restored 1915 Bing Crosby Theater is named for the Spokane-born singer. The INB Performing Arts Center is the city's premier entertainment venue. Regional history is on display at the **Northwest Museum of Arts & Culture★** (see Museums); its collections of Northern Plateau tribal art are comprehensive.

Washington Wine Country

East of the Cascade Range, at a similar latitude as the French wine regions of Bordeaux and Burgundy, sun-drenched arid valleys and rolling hills make ideal microclimates for growing grapes. With some 650 wineries, Washington's wine industry is the second in size after California. Eastern Washington holds 12 of the 13 AVAs (American Viticultural Area). The greatest concentration of wineries is found in and near Walla Walla, which boasts 100. Yakima Valley has more than 60 wineries. The new Lake Chelan AVA is among the most beautiful anywhere, with hillside wineries overlooking the deep sapphire waters of the lake. To learn more, visit www.washingtonwine.org.

Yakima Valley wine country

Courtesy of visityakimavalley.org

EASTERN WASHINGTON

87

YAKIMA VALLEY★

The agriculturally rich Yakima Valley stretches in a southeasterly arc nearly 100mi from Ellensburg to the Columbia River. The valley is the state's oldest and largest wine-growing region *(see sidebar)*. A commercial hub of 91,000 people, the city of Yakima holds a handful of wine-tasting rooms, and the historic North Front Street District, with cafes and boutiques. The **Yakima Valley Museum** *(2105 Tieton Dr.; 509-248-0747; www.yakimavalleymuseum. org)* showcases regional history, including native son US Supreme Court Justice **William O. Douglas** (1898-1980); and horse-drawn vehicles. The **Yakima Valley Trolleys Museum** *(306 W. Pine St.; 509-249-5962; www. yakimavalleytrolleys.org;)* is a depot for vintage electric trolley cars from the last interurban electric railroad in the nation; on summer weekends **trolley excursions** *($4)* are offered.

WALLA WALLA★

Lying 5mi north of the Oregon border, Walla Walla (pop. 32,000) is the epicenter of the state's

Walla Walla Main Street

©Tourism Walla Walla

booming wine tourism industry, surrounded by scores of vineyards and more than 100 wineries. Visitors can find plenty of lodging, as well as several wine-tasting rooms, upscale eateries and shops. An agricultural hub and college town, Walla Walla is also known for the Walla Walla **Sweet Onion**, a baseball-sized allium highly valued for its sweet flavor. The city originated as a Hudson's Bay Company outpost; Fort Walla Walla was a waypoint for Oregon Trail migrants. The original buildings are part of the **Fort Walla Walla Museum** *(See Historical Sites)*.

MUSEUMS

Maryhill Museum★

Rte. 14, 2mi west of Hwy. 97, 35 Maryhill Museum Dr., Goldendale. 509-773-3733. www.maryhillmuseum.org. Open mid-Mar–mid-Nov daily 10am-5pm. $9.

"What in Sam Hill is that?" onlookers wondered after the eccentric Seattle tycoon, who lent the phrase its name, built this concrete mansion in 1926. The baronial Beaux-Arts mansion sits on a high bluff overlooking the Columbia River. Hill's intent was to draw travelers to view his eclectic art collection. Opened to the public in 1940, the museum features Rodin sculptures, Art Nouveau glass and Native American artifacts, among other treasures. Nearby, a reproduction of Stonehenge looms over the arid landscape.

Northwest Museum of Arts & Culture★

2316 W. First Ave., Spokane. 509-456-3931. www.northwest museum.org. Open year-round Wed–Sat 10am–5pm (first Fri til 8pm). $7.

This affiliate of the Smithsonian Institution is the largest museum in the region. A splendid collection of artifacts from the **Plateau Indian culture** is supplemented by 10,000 photographs as well as contemporary works of art. The 1898 **Campbell House** sits adjacent to the museum.

Yakama Nation Museum★

About 15mi southeast of Yakima, 100 Spiel-yi Loop, in Toppenish. 509-865-2800. www.yakamamuseum. com. Open year-round Mon–Fri 8am–5pm, Sat–Sun 9am–5pm. $6.

The Yakama Nation Museum presents a trove of information and artifacts related to the history and culture of the **Yakama Indians**. Designed to represent a historic Yakama winter lodge, the 12,000sq-ft facility blends sights— including dramatic dioramas—and sounds to create the illusion of time travel from the historic past and continuing forward to today.

HISTORICAL SITES

Grand Coulee Dam★★

US 2, 88mi west of Spokane. 509-633-9265. www.usbr.gov/pn/ grandcoulee. Open late May–Jul daily 8:30am–11pm (til 10:30pm Aug, til 9:30pm Sept. Rest of the year hours vary.

This mammoth, 55-story wall of sloped concrete stretches across the **Columbia River** for nearly a mile, spanning the cliffs of a deep desert canyon. Built by the Civilian Conservation Corps in the 1930s to provide electricity for the state and irrigation for the dry Columbia Plateau, it is the largest concrete dam in North America and the third-largest electric power producer in the world. Free guided **tours** are available, and the nighttime **laser light show**, created by a company that has produced shows for Disneyland, is worth seeing.

Fort Walla Walla Museum★

755 Myra Rd., Walla Walla. 509-525-7703. www.fortwallawalla museum.org. Open Apr–Dec daily 10am–5pm. Rest of the year Sat–Sun 10am–4pm. $7.

Situated in a 70-acre wildlife preserve with streams and a multiuse trail, the museum consists of a **pioneer village** that evokes pioneer life in the Walla Walla region near the turn of the 20C. Original log buildings include a blacksmith, schoolhouse, jail, dentist shop and cabins, each filled with period furnishings and artifacts. The museum also has one of the nation's largest collections of horse-drawn **agricultural equipment**.

THE GREAT OUTDOORS

Lake Chelan★★

Hwy. 97, 103mi north of Ellensburg. 509-682-3503. www.lakechelan.com.

This narrow, 50mi-long lake is a recreational haven at its southern end, anchored by the tiny town of **Chelan**. At its northern end, wilderness terminates at the deeply forested community of **Stehekin**, a backpackers' launch pad into the rugged North Cascades National Forest. *The Lady of the Lake* passenger ferry and float planes carry travelers between the two points. In and near Chelan are pleasant beaches, including **Lake Chelan State Park**, with 6,000ft of shoreline. **Slidewaters** waterpark, in Chelan, offers another water-play option.

Dry Falls★

On Rte. 17, 17mi north of Soap Lake. www.parks.wa.gov. Open summer daily 6:30am–dusk. Winter 8am–dusk.

Few places offer as raw and memorable a look at geological forces as Dry Falls. The "falls" are a bowl-shaped 400ft chasm, 3.5mi wide, carved into volcanic bedrock in the Columbia Basin desert. Thousands of years ago, catastrophic Ice Age floods surged through here as prehistoric Lake Missoula in Montana periodically broke though its ice dam and sent billions of gallons of water west to the Pacific, carving the **Columbia Basin** landscape.

Lake Chelan

Courtesy of Lake Chelan Tourism

Manito Park★

1702 S. Grand Blvd., Spokane. 509-625-6200. www.spokaneparks.org. Open summer daily 4am–11pm. Winter 5am–10pm.

Two miles south of downtown, this park occupies 90 acres on Spokane's South Hill. Five themed gardens include a European Renaissance-style garden, a Japanese garden, a rose garden and a lilac garden.

The Palouse★

Rte.127 and Hwy. 2.

South of Spokane, rolling fields of grain resemble great sea swells in a region called the Palouse. The agricultural fields on the Palouse plateau are vivid green late March through June, and then turn golden in July as the wheat and safflower crops ripen. Country roads curve around bends throughout one of the finest areas anywhere for car touring. Some of the best scenery encompasses the small towns of Dayton and Pomeroy.

Off Highway 12, 69mi north of Walla Walla, **Palouse Falls★** plunges 180ft over a granite ledge into a deep chasm. The falls and canyon are a result of the Missoula Floods that periodically swept across the Columbia River Plateau in the Pleistocene era, creating channeled scablands.

Steptoe Butte★

12mi north of Colfax along US 195; turn east on Scholz Rd. 6mi north of Colfax. www.parks.wa.gov. Open year round 6am–dusk.

A 10min drive to the top of this solitary cone of ancient bedrock affords a 360-degree **view★★** of the Palouse region in Washington and Idaho. Rising 1,000ft, the 3,612ft butte is the highest point for miles around. On clear days the Cascades can be seen to the west, the Idaho Rockies to the east and Oregon's Blue Mountains to the south.

Yakima River Canyon★

Rte. 821, 10mi north of Yakima. www.blm.gov.

North of Yakima, the gentle Yakima River squeezes its namesake canyon, beneath 2,000ft-high basalt cliffs where golden eagles and red-tail hawks ride the thermals. State Route 821 offers a scenic corridor through the shrub-steppe habitat valley, notable for its rare plants. Rafting companies offer **float trips** down the scenic river. Either way, visitors are bound to see any of 21 species of raptors.

Hanford Reach National Monument

Various access points along the Columbia River and Rte. 225 north of Richland. 509-546-8300. www.fws.gov/hanfordreach. Open year-round daily dawn–dusk.

The last free-flowing interior stretch of the Columbia River winds through this sagebrush-dotted preserve between Richland and Wenatchee. The only facilities are boat launches, but it is a wildlife paradise, with deer, elk and birds seen while floating the 51mi stretch of river. Visitors also pass monoliths of recent history—the buildings that remain from World War II's Manhattan Project, which created the atom bomb. **Kayak tours** of the river are offered by Columbia Kayak Adventures *(509-947-5901; www.columbiakayakadventures.com; $115).*

Lake Roosevelt National Recreation Area

Rte. 25, milepost 23. 509-633-9441. www.nps.gov/laro.

Completion of the Grand Coulee Dam in 1941 created a 130mi long lake named for President Franklin D. Roosevelt. Boaters, fishers and outdoor enthusiasts frequent the sunny reservoir to camp, canoe and swim. Concessionaires rent watercraft, and even houseboats, at the 10 **swimming beaches** here.

Historic **Fort Spokane**, a military post and later an Indian boarding school, has a visitor center and **museum** open in summer *(daily 9:30am–5pm).*

PORTLAND★★

Lying about 175mi south of Seattle, Oregon's largest city dominates the northwest portion of the state. Hugging the banks of the Willamette River near its confluence with the Columbia River, Portland (pop: 594,000) is renowned for its urban wilderness, outdoors culture and rich culinary scene. Its proximity to spectacular natural wonders includes the rugged Columbia Gorge and Mount Hood to the east and Pacific Ocean beaches to the west. One of the most sustainable urban areas in the nation, it's a progressive, eco-minded city, with a first-rate transit system, a number of LEED-certified buildings, highly productive recycling and composting programs, and one of the largest farmers' markets in the country.

The city originated as a riverside stopping point for **Oregon Trail** travelers heading north to Fort Vancouver; it was known simply as "The Clearing." When it was incorporated in 1851, the city was less prosaically dubbed "Stumptown," for the landscape that persisted a little too long after logging. In the shadow of the territorial capital of Oregon City, 12mi south, Portland blossomed in the late 19C and early 20C due to the depth of the Columbia River, which supported ocean-going vessels.

In the dot-com boom of the 1990s, the siren call of nature, along with cheap rents and plentiful jobs

Fast Facts
Founded: 1845
Land area: 134sq mi
Population: 594,000 (metro 2.26 million)
Average annual precipitation: 37.5 inches
Average sunny days a year: 68

in Internet startups and graphic design drew large numbers of young people to Portland, and companies such as outdoor- and sports-gear makers Columbia, Nike and Adidas were at the forefront of Portland's industry. When the tech bubble burst, yet more

Portland skyline

© Robert Reynolds/Portland CVB

Practical Information

When to Go
From June through September, the weather in Portland tends to be consistently warm and pleasant, with average temperatures in July and August at around 80°F. This period is also **peak tourist season**, when the city's outdoor culture thrives. The Christmas holidays offer many cultural attractions as well as Mount Hood skiing nearby.

Getting There and Around
♦ **By Air** – **Portland International Airport** (PDX) (503-460-4040; www.flypdx.com) Is the region's major air hub.

♦ **By Train** – The city's historic Union Station is served by three intercity **Amtrak** (800-USA-RAIL; www.amtrak.com) routes providing daily service between Portland and Seattle, Vancouver, B.C. and Eugene.

♦ **By Light Rail** – Portland is famous for its superlative transportation system, and Tri-Met MAX Light Rail (503-238-7433; www.trimet.org/max) is the centerpiece, with 84 stations and 52mi of track connecting the city, airport and region; trains depart every 15min or sooner.

♦ **By Streetcar** – The **Portland Streetcar** (503-238-7433; www.trimet.org/streetcar) offers fast and efficient transportation throughout downtown; there are two lines, one north-south through downtown and a loop that crosses the Willamette River; streetcars come about every 15min all day.

♦ **By Car** – Portland is one of the few cities in the country where it's not necessary to use a private car, given the convenience of mass transit.

Visitor Information
Portland **visitor center** is located at 701 SW 6th Avenue (503-275-9750, www.TravelPortland.com).

artists were drawn to Portland for its comparatively low cost of living, helping to create a thriving performing and visual-arts focus. Today, the **Rose City** is especially beloved by young, artsy types who enjoy a tongue-in-cheek campaign to "Keep Portland Weird." Among its charms are a plethora of homegrown brewpubs and a burgeoning **food-cart scene** that has drawn international attention, and numerous cultural attractions and festivals—including the multi-faceted and popular **Rose Festival**, which culminates in the Grand Floral Parade in early June.

MAX Light Rail

©Tim Jewett/Portland CVB

PORTLAND

NEIGHBORHOODS

Downtown★

See map inside back cover.
Bounded by Willamette River on the
east and I-405 on the opposite side.

Portland's downtown, in the
southwest quadrant of the city,
encompasses two neighborhoods:
the **Pioneer District**, with high-
end retailers, department stores,
restaurants and hotels generally
centered on **Pioneer Courthouse
Square★**, and the **Cultural
District** (*bounded by SW Salmon S.,
SW Market St., SW Broadway and
SW 10th Ave*). Considered the city's
living room, the square hosts more
than 300 events each year; the
summer **Noon Tunes** series draws
visitors and office workers during
the lunch hour.

In December the **Holiday Ale
Festival** celebrates the city's taste
for specialty brews. The square is
also the convergence point for all
MAX light rail lines.

A few blocks northeast, the **Alder
Street Pod** (*Alder and Washington
Sts.*) is the city's largest assembly of
food carts, serving a kaleidoscope
of international fare.

South of the square, the
Cultural District is centered on
the 12-block-long **South Park
Blocks★**, a leafy oasis bordered
by museums and performing-arts
spaces, including the **Oregon
History Center**, the **Portland Art
Museum** and **Portland Center for
the Performing Arts**. The city's
largest farmers' market is held
here *(Wed)*. Beyond, the buildings
of **Portland State University's**
50-acre campus line both sides of
the Blocks, serving some 30,000
students.

Pearl District★

*Bounded by W. Burnside St., NW
Lovejoy St., NW 8th Ave. and NW
15th Ave.*

One of the hottest addresses in
town, The Pearl, in the northwest
corner, speaks to one of the
city's main tenets—re-purposing
industrial sites into functional
spaces. Today the neighborhood
brims with quirky boutiques,
art galleries, wine bars and
fashionable restaurants, many
inside historic brick buildings.

Meals on Wheels

Portland has numerous high-end restaurants attracting leading chefs
and sophisticated diners, yet it's the low-brow side of the city's dining
scene that has drawn national and international attention in recent
years. Portland is at the center of a burgeoning **food cart** scene, with an
astonishing 475 of them operating at any given time, selling everything
from Korean dumplings to Argentinian empanadas. This is not fair
food—many of the carts have won awards for their cuisine, and at
lunchtime lines wrap down the block at popular carts. While food carts
are dotted throughout the city, the best places to sample this cuisine is
at one of several food "pods," groupings of carts that offer a wide array
of choices. To learn more about the city's mobile food vendors, see
www.portlandfoodcarts.com.

In **Tanner Springs Park**, you can walk across a pond on a boardwalk, and **Jamison Square's** gushing fountain cascades down steps, filling a basin, and then retreats like the tide. Standouts are **Powell's City of Books** (see Shopping) the **Museum of Contemporary Craft** (see Museums); **Cargo**, a massive, vibrant shop whose owners travel the world, bringing back unique goods; and **BridgePort Brewing Co.**, known as much for innovative brews as for the party atmosphere inside the huge brick-and-timber building.

Portland Streetcar runs along the heart of the Pearl (10th and 11th Aves.). **First Thursday** gallery walk (www.firstthursdayportland.com) draws crowds to this fun, artsy district.

Old Town/Chinatown

Bounded by SW Naito Pkwy. SW Oak St., 3rd Ave. and NW Davis St.

The historic riverside district of Old Town contains within it the city's colorful **Chinatown** (bounded by NW 2nd and 5th Aves., W. Burnside and NW Glisan Sts.), the entrance to which is marked by the five-tiered **Chinatown Gate** Beneath the streets of both districts, **underground tunnels** were once used to "Shanghai" the unwary, carrying them off to servitude aboard ships. Today Old Town is a thriving dining and arts and entertainment district with one of the largest assemblages of **cast-iron buildings** in the nation. This district is also home to the city's über-popular **Saturday Market** (503-222-6072; www. portlandsaturdaymarket. com), now held Sundays too, the country's largest, continually operating open-air crafts market.

Chinatown's **Lan Su Chinese Garden** (see Parks and Gardens) is a lush walled space with pavilions reached by bridges and walkways in and around water features. Nearby, **Pendleton Woolen Mills'** flagship store (503-535-5444; www. pendleton-usa.com) stocks pricey but handsome Native American-inspired blankets in many patterns.

Northwest District

Around NW 23rd Avenue.

Portland's Nob Hill, which locals refer to as the **Northwest District**, bears many similarities to the famous Nob Hill in San Francisco. The narrow, tree-shaded streets are lined with lovingly restored Victorian homes and Craftsman dwellings turned into unique shopping spots, pubs and restaurants, including some of the best eateries in the city. The neighborhood is beloved by shoppers, who can easily access it via the Portland Streetcar. With sidewalk cafes and nightlife hot spots, Nob Hill bustles on summer evenings.

Northwest 23rd is the major shopping street, with **Northwest 21st** offering yet more retail, bars, and **Cinema 21**, the city's first-run art house movie theater (on Hoyt). The Northwest quadrant is also the setting for the grand, historic **Pittock Mansion**, as well as **Forest Park** (503-223-5449; www.forestparkconservancy.org), a 5,000- acre wilderness park, 8mi long, with 70mi of trails, in the Tualatin Mountains west of downtown.

MUSEUMS

Oregon History Center★★

1200 SW Park Ave. 503-222-1741.
www.ohs.org. Open year-round
Mon–Sat 10am–5pm,
Sun noon–5pm. $11.

Eight-story trompe l'oeil **murals**
of Lewis and Clark and the Oregon
Trail rise beside the entrance to
this archival museum. The **Oregon,
My Oregon** exhibit traces state
history, beginning with the 1840s
Oregon Trail migration. **Oregon
Voices★** presents stories from
1950 to today on interactive touch
screens, visitors can explore films,
photos and digital documents.

Portland Art Museum★★

1219 SW Park Ave. 503-226-2811.
www.pam.org. Open year-round
Tue–Sun 10am–5pm (til 8pm
Thu–Fri). $15.

The oldest (1892) art museum in
the Pacific Northwest occupies the
modernist-style Belluschi Building
and the historic Mark Building, as
well as an outdoor sculpture mall.
Highlights include the European

and East Asian galleries, the
Center for Northwest Art, which
brings regional artists to the fore,
including early 20C Oregon visitor
Childe Hassam and modern
master **Jacob Lawrence**, and the
Center for Native American Art.

Museum of Contemporary Craft

724 NW Davis St. 503-223-2654.
www.museumofcontemporary
craft.org. Open year-round Tue–
Sat 11am–6pm (til 8pm first Thu).
$4, free first Thu of month.

Bright, airy spaces in this two-story
museum consistently contain
provocative exhibits by artists of
national and international renown,
such as thought-provoking
contemporary works by world-
renowned Chinese artist **Ai
Weiwei**, and ceramics by Austrian-
born Otto and Gertrude Natzler.

World Forestry Center Discovery Museum

4033 SW Canyon Rd.,
Washington Park. 503-228-1367.
www.worldforestry.org. Open
year-round daily 10am–5pm. $9.

Following a major renovation in
2005, the World Forestry Museum
changed its name and its focus
from logging and forestry practices
to environmental sustainability
and the importance of forests
and wood products.
The first floor represents **Pacific
Northwest forests**; the second
floor allows visitors to "travel" to
Russia, China, South Africa and
Brazil to "see" their forests and
their challenges.

Portland Art Museum

©Bob Woodward/Portland CVB

MUST SEE PORTLAND

PARKS AND GARDENS

Lan Su Chinese Garden★★★

NW 3rd and Everett Sts. 503-228-8131. www.lansugarden.org. Open Apr–Oct daily 10am–6pm. Rest of the year til 5pm. $9.50.

Encompassing a city block, this 2000 addition to Portland's international district is a highly stylized retreat. Its high-walled courtyards, pools, walkways and pavilions are designed to mute the urban bustle outside its walls. Highlights inside the "Garden of Awakening Flowers" include a 7,000sq ft "lake" and Tai Hu limestone rocks, 500 tons of which were shipped here from China. Enjoy a respite in the **teahouse**.

Washington Park★★

Entrances south of W. Burnside Rd. and west of SW Vista Ave. 503-823-2525. www.washington parkpdx.org. Open year-round daily dawn–dusk.

This vast greensward serves as Portland's lung. The park is home to gardens, an arboretum, the **Oregon Zoo** (*opposite*), and **World Forestry Center** (*see Museums*). In a moist forest landscape laced with ponds, rivulets, artful bridges and stone pagodas, the 5.5-acre **Japanese Garden★★** (*611 SW Kingston Ave.; 503-223-1321; www.japanesegarden.com; open Apr–Sept Mon noon–7pm, Tue–Sun 10am–7pm; Oct–Mar til 4pm; $9.50*) offers reflective spaces in five distinct gardens: the Flat Garden, Strolling Pond Garden, Tea Garden, Natural Garden and Sand and Stone Garden.

At the **International Rose Test Garden★★★** (*400 SW Kingston Ave.; 503-823-3636; www.rosegarden store.org; open daily 7:30am–9pm*) clusters of pink, red and yellow roses (and other hues) spill down terraced hillsides with **Mount Hood** (*see The Great Outdoors*) in the distance. Some 10,000 bushes of 400 varieties grow here. A testing ground for new varieties, the garden is at its most resplendent June through September. Open-air concerts are held in August.

Just north of the Japanese Garden, the Château-style **Pittock Mansion★** (*3229 NW Pittock Dr.; 503-823-3623; www. pittockmansion.com; open Jul–Aug daily 10am–5pm; rest of year 11am–4pm; closed Jan; $8.50.*) perches on a 940ft crest in Imperial Heights. The 23-room manse was built in 1914 for a newspaper publisher.

Governor Tom McCall Waterfront Park★

Along the Willamette River between SW Harrison and NW Glisan sts. www.portland online.com.

This grassy, 30-acre park stretching along the Willamette River hosts numerous festivals throughout the year, and a natural amphitheater at the south end is the setting for outdoor concerts. Also at the south end, the **Portland Aerial Tram★** (*865- 8726; www.portlandtram.org*) offers visitors a view of the city and surrounding volcanic peaks during a 3min ride from the riverbank to Oregon Health Sciences University, on the bluff above.

FOR KIDS

🚢 Oregon Museum of Science and Industry★★

1945 SE Water Ave. 503-797-4000. www.omsi.edu. Open mid-Jun–Aug daily 9:30am–7pm. Rest of the year Tue–Sun 9:30am–5:30pm. $12., $9 children (ages 3-13).

This brick-and-glass building on the Willamette River incorporates an old power plant. Five halls, a 5-story Omnimax theater, a **planetarium** showing laser-light and other shows, and some 200 hands-on exhibits and labs explore everything from renewable energy and global climates to engineering and health and wellness. Outside, the retired non-nuclear **submarine** USS Blueback is open for tours *(45min)*.

Oregon Zoo★★

4001 SW Canyon Rd., Washington Park. 503-226-1561. www.oregonzoo.org. Open late May–early Sept daily 9am–6pm. Mid-Sept–Dec and Mar–mid-May til 4pm. Jan–Feb daily 10am–4pm. $10.50, children $7.50 (ages 3-11).

Set on a hillside, this excellent zoo houses most of its 2,200 animals in naturalistic enclosures. Large exhibit areas include the Great Northwest, Fragile Forests, Asia, Pacific Shores and Africa. A new exhibit focuses on endangered and threatened species such as the California condor.

Portland Children's Museum

4015 SW Canyon Rd., Washington Park. 503-223-6500.

Oregon Museum of Science and Industry

©OMSI

www.portlandcm.org. Open Mar–early Sept daily 9am–5pm (til 8pm Thu). Rest of the year Tue–Sun. $9, children $9 (ages 1 and older)

This excellent children's museum engages youth with a dozen hands-on learning exhibits. **Water Works** is a huge kid magnet, with waterwheels, boats to send down canals and lots of spraying and splashing. Other play areas are a "pet" hospital, a kid-size grocery store and a new, pint-sized maze.

Portland Timbers

JELD-WEN Field. 503-553-5400. www.portlandtimbers.com.

One of the newest Major League Soccer franchises, the Portland Timbers was launched in 2011 at JELD-WEN Field, a 20,000-seat built-for-soccer stadium. Home games are exciting affairs—the Timbers Army booster group keeps everyone, including children, on their feet singing and cheering.

THE GREAT OUTDOORS

🐾 Columbia Gorge★★

17mi east of Portland. 541-308-1700. www.fs.fed.us/r6/columbia.

The **Columbia River Gorge National Scenic Area★★** stretches about 80mi from Troutdale to the Deschutes River, encompassing 7 major waterfalls, 7 state parks and 700ft high cliff-edged views. The Columbia River creates fjord-like grandeur as it slices through a volcanic basalt gorge, with Oregon on the south bank and Washington on the north. En route, small towns attract visitors to local-food eateries, scenic lodging and varied recreation.

The historic 🐾 **Columbia River Highway★★** (US-30) offers a slower pace at which to enjoy the scenery; it's driveable in two sections linked by I-84. The 1916 **Vista House at Crown Point** *(Exit 22; www.vistahouse.com)*, an octagonal stone building on a cliff ledge 700ft above the river, is an interpretive center that offers an introduction to the Gorge; the eagle's eye **view★★** from here is worth a stop alone.

Just beyond, a series of waterfalls dash down mossy cliff sides. The **Multnomah Falls★★** *(Exit 31; 541-308-1700; www.fs.usda.gov)* plunge 620ft. An arching footbridge fords the stream between upper and lower falls; the 1925 **Multnomah Falls Lodge** is a splendid example of Cascadian-style architecture. While trails lead to the top and along the ridgeline of 90 falls along the Oregon side of the river, not all are easily accessed.

Past the cataracts, **Hood River** *(541-386-2000; www.hoodriver. org)* is a small town that's built its reputation on the nearly perpetual wind that blows here; it's at the apex of a world-renowned wind- and kite-surfing culture. Watching daredevils zip along the river, performing acrobatics as they near the shore can be thrilling. The town offers fine regional restaurants and lodging, as well as brewpubs and a growing wine industry, with many of the businesses tucked inside historic brick buildings.

During harvest season, valley farms along the 35mi 🐾 **Hood River County Fruit Loop** *(541-386-7697; www.hoodriverfruitloop.com)* scenic drive throw their gates open to visitors; you're likely to find farm-fresh wares, from alpaca knits and lavender-scented lotions, to apple pies and fine wines.

East of Hood River some 18mi, the **Columbia Gorge Discovery Center** *(541-296-8600; www.gorge discovery.org)*, in the town of

Flight of the Swifts

Every September evening, one hour before sunset, swarms of humans gather to watch flocks of birds—thousands of migratory **Vaux's Swifts**—as they dive inside a chimney at **Chapman Elementary School** *(1445 NW 26th Ave.)*. The birds use the chimney as a roosting spot during their fall migration. The event is a community ritual that elicits cheers from bystanders and picnickers. **Portland Audubon Society** members are among the crowd, answering questions.

Mount Hood

The Dalles explores the geologic beginnings of the gorge, the Native Americans and early settlers who called this region home, and modern regional developments. **The Dalles** refers also to the remarkable other-worldly terrain of gutter-like stone formations rising east of town.

⛷ Mount Hood★★

US-26, 50mi east of Portland. 503-622-3017. www.mthood.org.

The snow-clad cone of Oregon's highest peak pierces the clouds at 11,249 ft. Topped with a dozen glaciers, the **stratovolcano** is a backyard recreational mecca for Portland residents who get away to its forested slopes for hiking or ⛷ **skiing**.

Below the Palmer Glacier, but sitting at the 6,000ft timberline, **Timberline Lodge★** *(off US-26; 503-272-3311; www.timberline lodge.com)* is a national historic landmark built by the Works Progress Administration in 1936-1937; it's a fine example of American craftsmanship using native stone and local fir and pine. The spacious hexagonal **lobby** has oak floors with wooden pegs, and a massive stone chimney rising 92ft.

The Timberline ski area **Palmer Express ski lift** carries skiers 1,500 feet farther up the mountain, depositing them on the Palmer snowfield, with broad, open southern views of the Cascade Mountains; the Timberline ski area is the only year-round ski operation in North America, with 3,690 vertical feet of skiing and snowboarding.

Seven miles west, the **Mount Hood Skibowl** *(503-272-3206; www.skibowl.com)* is the mountain's largest ski operation. In summertime the mountain is a recreational playground as well. The Mount Hood Skibowl becomes the **Mount Hood Adventure Park**, with mountain biking, bungee jumping, zip lines and other activities, and mountain hiking includes the spectacular 40mi-long **Timberline Trail★★**.

PERFORMING ARTS

Artists Repertory Theatre

1515 SW Morrison St. 503-241-1278. www.artistsrep.org

This company's resident actors stage contemporary and classic productions throughout the season in two intimate venues.

Oregon Ballet Theatre

1111 SW Broadway. 503-222-5538. www.obt.org.

Company dancers perform five works a season, including classics, 20C masterpieces and contemporary works, at the **Portland Center for the Performing Arts**.
The company is particularly noted for its inventory of George Balanchine ballets.

SHOPPING

Lloyd Center

NE 9th Ave. and Multnomah. 503-282-2511. www.lloydcenter.com.

Oregon's largest mall is home to almost 200 shops, as well as an 8-screen movie theater and an indoor **ice rink**, reachable from downtown via MAX light rail.

🛍 Nob Hill / NW 23rd

Along NW 21st and NW 23rd Sts. www.nobhillbiz.com.

This neighborhood has specialty shops selling jewelry and high-end kitchenware to handmade apparel, you name it. Pottery Barn and Restoration Hardware also here.

Oregon Symphony

1037 SW Broadway. 503-228-1353. www.orsymphony.org.

Founded in 1896, the symphony performs the classics and pops at the Arlene Schnitzer Concert Hall.

Portland Center Stage

128 NW 11th Ave. 503-445-3700. www.pcs.org.

The Gerding Theater and Ellyn Bye Studio are the venues here for both large and intimate productions.

Portland Opera

222 SW Clay St. 503-241-1407. www.portlandopera.org.

Keller Auditorium at the Portland Center for the Performing Arts is this innovative opera's home.

Touring Tip

Thanks to tax-free retail, Portland is a major shopping destination.

811 Design Center

811 E. Burnside St.

Coming across this shopping center is a surprise—it's a counter-culture "mall" of indie boutiques inside a multistory brick building. The shops here are filled with locally designed apparel and accessories from designers such as Nationale and Haunt, alongside vintage clothing and creative services, like graphic designers and local artists.

PERFORMING ARTS/SHOPPING

⚓ Pearl District

Bounded by W. Burnside, the Willamette River, I-405 and NW Broadway. 503-227-8519. www.explorethepearl.com.

This renovated area of town, originally 20C brick warehouses, houses local-goods boutiques and art galleries, alongside restaurants and wine bars. The Pearl is full of surprises, such as the antique letterpresses in operation at **Oblation Papers and Press**. Major retailers Patagonia, Filson, Keen Footwear and others are here. Small parks nearby offer respite.

Powell's City of Books

1005 W. Burnside; 503-228-4651; www.powells.com.

Book-lovers and the curious alike are fascinated by Powell's, which encompasses an entire block and stocks 1 million-plus titles. First in the US to mix used and new books on its shelves, the pioneering bookseller today is widely considered the world's largest single bookstore. Some 6,000 daily visitors need store maps to navigate the maze of color-coded rooms and sections.

NIGHTLIFE

Aladdin Theater

3017 SE Milwaukie Ave. 503-234-9694. www.aladdin-theater.com.

This 620-seat space, once a vaudeville venue, still has a 1920s vibe. Renowned for excellent acoustics, The Aladdin books national touring acts ranging from jazz, blues and pop to world music.

⚓ Crystal Ballroom

1332 W Burnside St. 503-225-0047. www.mcmenamins.com.

Built in 1914 as a dance pavilion, the venue today features a broad range of musical artists, from folk musicians to hard-edged rock acts. The third-floor space, renovated by McMenamin's, opened in the late '90s with soaring ceilings, sparkling chandeliers and murals. Below the ballroom, **Lola's Room** hosts DJ dances and local rock bands, and beneath Lola's, Ringler's Pub offers pints and Northwest pub fare.

Doug Fir Lounge

830 E Burnside. 503-231-9663. www.dougfirlounge.com.

Portland's hipster culture is in full bloom at the Doug Fir Lounge, with its retro ski cabin ambiance and focus on indie-alt and avant-garde music. The onsite **restaurant** serves American comfort food fare until the wee hours.

⚓ Jimmy Mak's

221 NW 10th Ave. 503-295-6542. www.jimmymaks.com.

The city's premier jazz club, Jimmy Mak's is a richly decorated, sophisticated space that hosts local and national jazz acts every night of the week. With a menu of Greek and Middle Eastern–style dishes adding to the experience, Jimmy Mak's is a popular date-night venue.

WILLAMETTE VALLEY ★

The broad, fertile Willamette Valley runs north to south 110 miles from Portland to Eugene at its southern edge. This valley was the promised land that began attracting pioneers via the Oregon Trail in the 1840s. Today, despite being the state's most populated region outside metropolitan Portland, much of the area retains a rural feel, set as it is with farmland, tulip fields, hazelnut orchards and covered bridges. The pride of Oregon, the valley is one of the richest agricultural regions in the country.

The Willamette's **loamy soil** gives rise to a feast of foods that enrich the plates of the finest restaurants in Portland. The climate and soil are ideal for **vineyards**, and more than 🍇 **500 wineries**, mostly west of Interstate 5, draw visitors from around the world to wine-country tasting rooms. Charming small towns, bucolic countryside and **farm stands** provide additional reasons to stop and savor Oregon's wine country.

A string of cities, including the **state capital** of Salem and the free-spirited town of Eugene, are situated along I-5, which runs north to south through the center of the valley. To the west, the forested **Coast Range** cradles the valley, and 30mi to the east, waterfalls plummet down mossy Cascade Range hillsides alongside wooded 🥾 **hiking** trails whose vine maple trees turn crimson and orange in the fall.

CITIES

SALEM ★

The **capital** of Oregon is the state's third-largest city (pop. 156,000). Salem traces its founding to 1840, when Jason Lee moved the headquarters of his Methodist mission to this mid Willamette Valley location. Lee's house and other early buildings still stand at the **Willamette Heritage Center at the Mill ★★** *(1313 Mill St.; 503-585-7012; www.willametteheritage. org; open year-round Mon–Sat 10am–5pm ;$6)*, a five-acre historical park that includes the 1889 **Thomas Kay Woolen Mill**. A millstream courses beneath the main mill building, and inside, massive looms operate with water-powered turbines. Four buildings,

filled with period furnishings, were moved to this site, and are considered the oldest in the Northwest, dating to the 1840s. Downtown, the domed **Oregon State Capitol ★** *(bounded by Court, Capitol, State and Cottage Sts.; 503-986-1388; www.leg.state. or.us)*, built in 1938 in the Greek Revival style, is topped by a 23ft statue of a pioneer. The capitol and its grounds are some of the finest anywhere, with broad lawns, fountains, statues, and murals that tell the tale of the first pioneers who came west on wagon trains. Just south, the 90-acre **Bush's Pasture Park** centers on a Victorian house-turned-museum; the park also holds the state's

Practical Information

When to Go

Spring through fall, the Willamette Valley is impressive. In May and June, Cascade waterfalls are at their peak flow, gardens are in bloom and temperatures are moderate. July through September the weather is warm and pleasant, with an average of 83°F in August. Late September and October is grape crush time at valley vineyards and fall foliage season in the Cascades.

Getting There and Around

♦ **By Air** – **Portland International Airport** (PDX) (503-460-4040; www.flypdx.com) is the region's major air hub.

♦ **By Train** – **Amtrak** (800-USA-RAIL; www.amtrak.com) provides daily service between Portland and Salem, Albany and Eugene.

♦ **By Bus** – **Greyhound** (214-849-8966; www.greyhound.com) provides regularly scheduled bus service to communities throughout the Willamette Valley.

♦ **By Car** – It's easiest to reach Willamette Valley destinations with a private vehicle; all the major car-rental agencies can be found at Portland International Airport.

Visitor Information

To learn more about Willamette Valley sights, call 503-378-8850 or visit www.traveloregon.com or the **Willamette Valley Visitors Association** (866-548-5018; www.oregonwinecountry.org).

oldest greenhouse conservatory, as well as gardens and trails. Just west, **Riverfront Park** is home to the artful **Riverfront Carousel**, with wooden animals hand-carved by volunteers, and **A.C. Gilbert's Discovery Village★** (*see For Kids*).

ALBANY

Sitting at the center of Willamette Valley, this pleasant small town (pop. 51,000) has a historic aura about it. Its neighborhoods are filled with 700-plus heritage buildings, from Craftsman

Willamette Valley vineyard

©Rachel Coe

Oregon Wine Country

Situated on the same latitude as France's Burgundy region, the **Willamette Valley** has developed into one of the finest viticultural regions in the world. Today, Oregon boasts more than 500 wineries *(Oregon Wine Country: 503-228-8336; www.oregonwine.org)*. Several small towns here make good bases for exploration. **Newberg** is quaint, with a tiny downtown, yet it is home to the **Allison Inn & Spa** *(503-554-2525; www.theallison.com)*, a hillside property with a spa and one of the best regional restaurants in the state, Jory; downtown, **The Painted Lady** *(503-538-3850; www.thepaintedladyrestaurant.com)*, inside a Victorian, also draws foodies from near and far. The hamlet of **Carlton** features B&Bs and historic inns, as well as wine-tasting rooms, a handcrafted chocolate shop and several cafes. **McMinnville** is considered one of the nation's most exciting food towns, with wine bars and cafes tucked into late 19C buildings, alongside boutiques and antiques shops. On main street, **McMenamins' Hotel Oregon** *(503-472-8427; www.mcmenamins.com)*, in a historic, 4-story brick building, attracts wine-country visitors and revelers to its three bars. Nearby, the **Evergreen Aviation & Space Museum** *(see Museums)* and **Wings and Waves Waterpark** *(503-434-4185; www.evergreenmuseum.org)* draw aviation buffs and water-lovers.

bungalows to Queen Anne Victorian homes, as well as the 1849 **Monteith House★** *(518 2nd Ave.; 541-928-0911; www.albanyvisitors.com)*, a house museum filled with period artifacts, and listed on the National Register of Historic Places. The **Albany Historic Carousel and Museum** *(see Museums)* is new.

EUGENE

Known as Track Town USA, Eugene is an outdoors-centric town that has given rise to the Nike company, as well as to many Olympics runners. The city is also home to the University of Oregon, whose excellent **Jordan Schnitzer Museum of Art★★** *(see Museums)* is a fantasy of intricate brickwork built for a massive collection of Asian art. Also on campus, the **Museum of Natural and Cultural History★** *(541-346-3024; natural-history.uoregon.edu)* which

doubled in size in 2013, has a new, exhibit, "Explore Oregon!" focusing on volcanoes, earthquakes and tsunamis, as well as evolution and environmental stewardship. In the 1960s and 70s, U of O "radicals" backed a strong countercultural scene, leading to a wave of organic food stores, green living and tie-dyed clothing. Today vestiges of Eugene's colorful past remain in tie-dyed garments for sale at the **Saturday Market** *(8th and Oak downtown; Apr–Nov)*; it's the oldest open-air crafts market in the nation. The July **Oregon Country Fair** *(www.oregoncountryfair.org)*, in the town of Veneta, 15mi west of Eugene, still attracts aging hippies driving hand-painted VW vans. Many Eugene restaurants serve local, sustainably grown foods. For a town of 157,000, the quality of dining experience is excellent: local companies produce yogurt, cheese, coffee, chocolate and wine.

MUSEUMS

Evergreen Aviation & Space Museum★★

500 NE Captain Michael King Smith Way, McMinnville. 503-434-4185. www.evergreenmuseum.org. Open year-round daily 9am–5pm. $20.

The centerpiece of this experiential aviation museum is the **Spruce Goose**, a World War II plane that was built entirely of wood because of wartime restrictions on metal. Additional displays include one of the world's fastest aircraft, the SR-71 Blackbird, and the Titan II missile. The complex also includes a theater showing mostly flight-inspired movies, and the new **Wings and Waves Waterpark**, which has drawn rave reviews for its splashy features.

Jordan Schnitzer Museum of Art★★

1430 Johnson Lane, Eugene. 541-346-3027. jsma.uoregon. edu. Open year-round Tue–Sun 11am–5pm, (til 8pm Wed). $5, free first Fri of the month.

This expansive museum, built in 1933 to hold a 3,700-piece collection of Oriental art, continues its focus on Asian art, particularly ancient and modern Japanese and Korean art. The Schnitzer also holds one of the largest collections of works by Northwest expressionist painter **Morris Graves**, as well as works by his contemporaries. In the Russian Gallery, **orthodox icons** from the 15C to the 20C are on view in rotation.

©Albany Visitors Association

Quigga the Quagga and admirer, Albany Historic Carousel and Museum

Albany Historic Carousel and Museum

501 1st Ave. W, Albany. 541-791-3340. www.albanycarousel. com. Open year-round Mon–Sat 10am–4pm (til 9pm Wed).

Located in the city's historic section, this new museum has been a work in progress for many years. The town's residents are building a Dentzel-style **carousel** by hand, carving, sanding and painting wooden animals.

Hallie Ford Museum of Art★

On the campus of Willamette University, 700 State St., Salem 503-370-6855. www.willamette.edu. Open year-round Tue–Sat 10am–5pm, Sun 1pm–5pm. $3.

This well-regarded small museum has a diverse collection that spans Europe, Asia and North America; it's focus is on regional **Northwest works** and traditional Native American **basketry**.

WILLAMETTE VALLEY

MUST SEE

THE GREAT OUTDOORS

The Oregon Garden★★

879 W Main St., Silverton. 503-874-8100. www.oregongarden.org. Open May–Sept daily 9am–6pm. Rest of the year daily 10am–4pm. $11.

More than 20 gardens and features on 80 acres offer sensory delights at The Oregon Garden. A stroll through its network of pathways leads past ponds and waterfalls, a **Northwest Garden**, a Children's Garden and many other plant-filled nooks.
The site also includes two pieces of history: the Willamette Valley's natural habitat of **oak prairie**, which has nearly disappeared, can be seen in an oak grove, whose crowning jewel is the **Heritage Tree**, which is more than 400 years old.
In addition, Frank Lloyd Wright's 1957 **Gordon House**, relocated to The Oregon Garden in 2002, is the only such Northwest house open to the public; tours are available by advance reservation only.

Trail of Ten Falls★★

Silver Falls State Park, Hwy. 214, 26 mi east of Salem. 503-73-8681. www.oregonstateparks.org. Open daily year-round.

On the western slope of the Cascade Range, 8,700-acre **Silver Falls State Park** is Oregon's largest such park. It is home to one of the state's best hikes: an 8mi **hiking trail** that passes 10 waterfalls plunging off basalt ledges, the highest of which is 177ft **South Falls**. The park's 25mi of trails traverse Douglas-fir and western hemlock forests with a thick understory of sword fern, salal and Oregon grape (a grape in name only).

Cascades Raptor Center

32275 Fox Hollow Rd., Eugene. 541-485-1320. www.eraptors.org. Open Apr–Oct Tue–Sun 10am–6pm. Rest of the year 10am–4pm. $7.

This hillside nature center is a rescue facility for wounded birds

The Oregon Garden

Owl, Cascades Raptor Center

Eugene, Cascades & Coast

from throughout the Northwest. The center's special focus is birds of prey; more than 50 resident birds of scores of species, including owls, falcons, hawks, ospreys and bald eagles, are housed in spacious cages reached via meandering pathways. The weekend **handler talks** offer visitors the best opportunity to learn more about these amazing creatures.

FOR KIDS

A.C. Gilbert's Discovery Village★

116 Marion St. NE, Salem. 503-371-3631; www.acgilbert.org. Open year-round Mon–Sat 10am–5pm, Sun noon–5pm. $7, $2 children (age 2 and under).

Housed inside three historic homes, this excellent hands-on children's museum is known for its American Flyer S-gauge trains, a bubble room and an immense 20,000sq ft outdoor play area.

The Enchanted Forest

©Travel Salem

The Enchanted Forest

8462 Enchanted Way SE, Turner. 503-371-4242; www.enchanted forest.com. Open late May–early Sep daily 10am–6pm; closed Dec–mid-Mar; rest of the year, hours vary. $10.95, $9.95 children (ages 3-12). Rides 95 cents each (height limits apply).

Located 10mi south of Salem, this family-owned **theme park** sits in a forest. Among the kid-pleasers are Storybook Lane and Tofteville Western Town. Favorite rides include the Big Timber Log Ride, and Ice Mountain bobsleds.

Science Factory Children's Museum & Exploration Dome

2300 Leo Harris Pkwy, Eugene. 541-682-7888. www.science factory.org. Open year-round Wed–Sun 10am–4pm (dome Sat–Sun only). $7, $4 exhibits only.

For tots to pre-teens, this museum, in Alton Baker Park, is a modest, but lively, place with engaging exhibits and a planetarium.

WILLAMETTE VALLEY

MUST DO

OREGON COAST

Along the 362mi wind-buffeted Oregon Coast, the terrain sports as many moods as the weather. Beginning at the Columbia River, the North Coast is lined with long, golden-sand beaches snugged against forested hillsides. Gnarly and muscular, the Central Coast is filled with rocky headlands and sea stacks bracing against the wind and waves, yet pocketed with calm bays. On the South Coast, the landscape shifts again to miles of beaches, some with towering dunes. The entire coast, though, is one big playground perfect for kite flying, picnicking and viewing wildlife. The string of towns stretching along the shore offer scenic lodgings, quaint shops selling locally crafted art, and countless restaurants serving up the riches of the sea.

The lush landscape has attracted human settlement for thousands of years. Fish, mussels, berries, crabs, elk—the bounty of the sea and the forest—plus a mild climate enabled **coastal tribes** to establish permanent villages and thrive. European explorers sailed along the Oregon shores as early as 1543, but it was not until the 18C that sea otter and beaver pelts drew attention. The coastal towns that sprung up weren't fully connected to the outside world until the completion in the 1930s of Highway 101 along the coast.

Passport to Adventure

A number of exceptionally beautiful places along the Oregon Coast, including Shore Acres State Park, Cape Perpetua and Yaquina Head, require day-use fees. The 5-day **Oregon Pacific Coast Passport** ($10) offers entry to 8 day-use coastal parks, including Fort Clatsop and Oregon Dunes NRA. To learn more about the pass and how to buy it, access www.fs.usda.gov.

Looking south from Ecola State Park

©Peter Wrenn/Michelin

OREGON COAST

Practical Information

When to Go

Coastal temperatures are always mild, ranging from the 50°Fs to the 70°Fs. In summer, weather here is highly unpredictable, with either fog or sunshine. Peak season brings an abundance of tourists, however, and, with no direct route, traffic is typically heavy and slow. Many consider September the best time to visit the coast.

Getting There and Around

◆ **By Air** – **Portland International Airport** (PDX) (503 460-4040; www.flypdx.com) is the closest air hub for travelers visiting Oregon's North Coast. The **Eugene Airport** (EUG) (541-682-5430; www.flyeug. com) is the closest airport to the Central Coast, and the **Rogue Valley International-Medford Airport** (MFR) (541-772-8068; www.co.jackson.or.us) is the closest airport to the South Coast. Rental-car agencies are available at all three airports.

◆ **By Bus** – **Greyhound** (214-849-8100; www.greyhound.com) serves select communities along the Oregon Coast.

◆ **By Car** – It's easiest to see Oregon Coast sights by private car; all regional airports have major car-rental agencies.

Visitor Information

To learn about the Oregon Coast, call 541-574-2679 or access www.visittheoregoncoast.com. Additional tourism sites include: **Astoria** (503-325-6311; www.oldoregon.com); **Cannon Beach**, (503-436-2623; www.cannonbeach.org); **Newport** (541-265-8801; www.discovernewport.com); and **Coos Bay** (541-269-0215; www.oregonsadventurecoast.com).

CITIES

ASTORIA★★

Situated at the confluence of the Columbia River and the Pacific Ocean, this town of 10,000 is the oldest settlement west of the Rocky Mountains. Founded in 1811 as a **fur-trading post**, Astoria had become, by the late 1880s, an important port and the site of numerous salmon canneries. Astoria evokes the past—with Victorian houses stair-stepping down steep, forested hillsides and a 1920s-era downtown.

On the waterfront, the **Columbia River Maritime Museum** (*see Museums*) focuses on the region's maritime heritage, including the hazards of the nearby Columbia River Bar, where the Columbia meets the Pacific. Large standing waves here create dangerous conditions for navigation, and the area is known worldwide as the "Graveyard of the Pacific" for its many **shipwrecks**.

The museum is located on the 5mi **Riverwalk**, a water-side path; the **Astoria Riverfront Trolley** (*$1*), whose conductors share local lore, runs alongside the trail. To the south, the 1926 **Astoria Column**, crowning a 600ft hill, resembles Trajan's Column in Rome; it's open to those who climb 164 stairs to the top, from which **views** take in the Pacific Ocean and the **Astoria-Megler Bridge**, the largest truss bridge in the world, to the west. For history buffs, the **Clatsop County Historical Society** *(503-325-2203; www.cumtux.org)* offers tours of the **Flavel House**, an 1886 Queen Anne Victorian with period furnishings; and the **Heritage Museum**, housed in the old city hall, has exhibits ranging from Indian baskets to a partial reconstruction of an early saloon. **Fort Clatsop**, 6mi southwest, preserves the site where Lewis and Clark spent the winter of 1805-06 (*see Historical Site*).

CANNON BEACH★

This charming hamlet of 2,000 inhabitants caters to artists and well-heeled visitors from Portland, 80mi east. Shops, galleries, cafes and cozy hostelries compete for attention with the expansive sand beach, backed by iconic **Haystack Rock,** which rises 235ft at the water's edge.

NEWPORT★

Edging the Central Coast, this town (pop: 10,000) sits at the center of a ruggedly beautiful region of cliffs, beaches and Oregon's famous **sea stacks**—large rock formations, often pillar-shaped that rise out of the ocean close to shore. Spreading out along Southwest Bay Boulevard, near mammoth **Yaquina Bay Bridge**, Newport's **Historic Bayfront District** is filled with shops, seafood restaurants and fishing-charter operations. The lively scene offers views of fishing boats coming and going, as well as docks filled with noisy sea lions.

🐋 Whale of a Time

An astonishing 18,000 **gray whales** pass the Oregon Coast annually on their 12,000mi migration between the Arctic and the warm waters off Mexico. Trained volunteers are stationed at 24 coastal sites like **Cape Perpetua Interpretive Center** and **Sea Lion Caves** to help visitors spy the leviathans in winter *(last week of the year)* and spring *(last week of Mar)*. See www.oregon.gov/oprd/parks/whalewatchingcenter for details.

The town is a favorite among families for the **Oregon Coast Aquarium** (*see For Kids*), rated among the top aquariums in the country.
Four miles up the coast, the **Yaquina Head** natural area (*see The Great Outdoors*) occupies an ancient finger of lava that protrudes into the Pacific.

COOS BAY

The largest natural deep-water harbor between Puget Sound and San Francisco Bay, Coos Bay, on Oregon's South Coast, is a commercial and shipping center with 16,000 residents. The town attracts tourists to its waterfront boardwalk, shops and galleries, as well as to the **Coos Art Museum** *(541-267-3901; www.coosart.org)*, which specializes in Northwest art. The bay is situated between **Oregon Dunes National Recreation Area** to the north and **Shore Acres State Park**, 13mi to the south.

MUSEUMS

Columbia River Maritime Museum★

1792 Marine Dr., Astoria. 503-325-2323. www.crmm.org. Open year-round daily 9:30am–5pm. $12.

To reach Columbia River ports, ships must survive the immense waves of the **Columbia River Bar**, the point where the river collides with the Pacific Ocean; these monster waves can tower as high as 40ft during storms. Located near the confluence, the museum features large windows that overlook ships and barges powering past. Interactive displays and actual **rescue vessels** induce a healthy dose of respect for seafarers. In the **tugboat simulator**, visitors can experience what it's like to pilot these dangerous waters.

Tillamook Air Museum

6030 Hangar Rd.,Tillamook. 503-842-1130. www.tillamookair.com. Open year-round daily 9am–5pm. $9.

Located in the inland town of Tillamook, 41mi south of Cannon Beach, this museum, housed in an immense WWII blimp hangar, features more than 30 restored **military aircraft**. Aviation artifacts and a 1950s-style cafe recall the wartime era.

HISTORICAL SITE

Fort Clatsop★★

92343 Fort Clatsop Rd., Astoria. 503-861-2471. www.nps.gov/lewi. Open mid-Jun–early Sept daily 9am–6pm. Rest of year daily 9am–5pm. $3.

Fort Clatsop was the winter encampment of Lewis and Clark's Corps of Discovery from 1805 to 1806. Today's visitors can explore a re-creation of the stockade at the **interpretive center**, which is the primary hub for the park.
In 1805 US President Thomas Jefferson dispatched **William Clark** and **Meriwether Lewis** to explore the lands of the newly acquired **Louisiana Purchase**. Known as the **Corps of Discovery**, a contingent of 31 men—mostly US army enlistees—crossed some 4,000mi of North America overland, mapping and observing the Native American tribes, plants and animals as it went. Near present-day **Astoria**, the end of their journey, they established a rustic camp, Fort Clatsop, named for a local Indian tribe. Despite spending a "wet, cold, and disagreeable" winter there, Clark described parts of the Pacific coastline as "the grandest and most pleasing prospects."
To maximize your visit, view the 12min film "A Clatsop Winter Tale" in the interpretive center; see the artifacts on exhibit, such as a 1795 musket, a bear-hide quiver and reproduced journal entries; and wander through the **full-size replica** of Fort Clatsop.

OREGON COAST

MUST SEE

THE GREAT OUTDOORS

Oregon Dunes National Recreation Area★★★

855 Highway Ave., Reedsport. 541-271-6000. www.fs.fed.us/ r6/siuslaw. Open Jul–early Sept Mon–Sat 8am–4:30pm. Rest of year Mon–Fri 8am–4:30pm.

Between Florence and Coos Bay, this 40mi strand of **coastal dunes**, some as high as 200ft, offers an ecosystem of sand, tree islands, wetlands, estuaries and beaches. At the **Oregon Dunes Visitor Center** at the north end of Reedsport, a range of exhibits and a movie provide orientation, and rangers direct travelers to trails and overlooks. The **Umpqua Scenic Dunes Trail★★**, 11mi south of Reedsport, features a half-mile path to the ocean.

Cape Perpetua Scenic Area★★

Central Coast, 2mi south of Yachats. 541-750-7000. www.fs.usda.gov. $5/vehicle.

The spectacular headlands of Cape Perpetua offer some of the most dramatic views on the coast. Trails through wind-sculpted spruce trees lead to a jagged, volcanic shoreline riddled with cracks and channels that concentrate the waves' power. **Spouting Horn** and **Devils Churn**, reached by trails, put on exciting shows during high tide. During low tide, **tide pools** are windows into tiny worlds of vividly colored sea anemones and sea stars. The 27,000-acre park also boasts a total of 27mi of trails and immense stands of **old-growth forest**.

Bright Lights

The Oregon coastline is dotted with 11 **lighthouses**. Nine of them are considered historic, but all are definitely photogenic structures on sweeping headlands with phenomenal views.

Heceta Head, on a 150ft bluff, is widely considered as one of the most beautiful lighthouses in the world; the lighthouse and keeper's house (now a B&B) date to 1894. For information about viewing or touring Oregon's lighthouses, access www. visittheoregoncoast.com.

Yaquina Head Outstanding Natural Area★★

750 NW Lighthouse Dr., Newport. 541-574-3100. www.blm.gov. Interpretive center open Jun–Aug daily 10am–6pm; Sept til 5pm; Oct–May til 4:30pm. $5/vehicle.

Covering a narrow, mile-long peninsula jutting into the Pacific Ocean north of Newport, this natural area is one of the most accessible wildlife locales on the Oregon Coast. For a phenomenal ocean **view**, climb the 110 steps of the 93ft-high **Yaquina Head Lighthouse★** (1872), Oregon's tallest operating lighthouse. At low tide, some of the coast's best **tide pools** are visible. Ranger-led tours of tide pools and lighthouse are offered in summer.

PARKS AND GARDENS

Ecola State Park★★

US Hwy 101, 2mi north of Cannon Beach. $5/vehicle. 503-436-2844. www.oregonstateparks.org.

This spectacularly scenic park, visited by Lewis and Clark, wraps around **Tillamook Head** and takes in 9mi of Pacific Ocean shoreline. Trails here, many of them through dense old-growth forest, include an 8mi section of the **Oregon Coast Trail**. Indian Beach is the starting point for a new, 2.5mi interpretive trail. The park is revered for its whale-watching overlooks, as well as for surfing and beachcombing.

Cape Arago State Park★

Off US 101, 14mi southwest of Coos Bay. 541-888-3778. www.oregonstateparks.org. Open year-round daily dawn–dusk.

At this park it's common to sight whales, seals and sea lions from the 150ft bluffs; the beach below harbors **tide pools** filled with intertidal plants and animals.

Oswald West State Park★

US 101, 10mi south of Cannon Beach. 541-888-8867. www.oregonstateparks.org.

This park is among the most scenic coastal parks in the state. Trails, including a 13mi section of the **Oregon Coast Trail,** meander through old-growth forest; some trails culminate on coastal headlands. The secluded **Short Sands Beach**, tucked into bluff-embraced Smugglers Cove, is beloved by surfboarders, white-water kayakers and picnickers.

Shore Acres State Park★

Off US 101, 13mi southwest of Coos Bay. 866-888-6100. www.shoreacres.net. Open year-round daily 8am–dusk. $5.

This park, originally a pioneer estate, features a 5-acre cliff-top botanical garden with flowers from around the world, two rose gardens, and one of the largest Monterey pines in the world.

Oswald West State Park

©Peter Wrenn/Michelin

FOR KIDS

Oregon Coast Aquarium★★

2820 SE Ferry Slip Rd., Newport. 541-867-3474. www.aquarium.org. Open late May–early Sept daily 9am–6pm. Rest of year daily 9am–5pm. $18.95, $11.95 children.

This excellent aquarium, among the top such such facilities in the nation, features five major indoor galleries and six acres of outdoor exhibits. With minor exceptions, the nearly 200 species are native to the coastal waters of Oregon. The aquarium complements its exhibits with a hands-on lab, an estuary trail and a theater.

In the immensely popular **Passages of the Deep** exhibit, visitors walk through a 200ft **glass tunnel** surrounded by Oregon Coast sealife, some five species of shark among the marine creatures on view. Other key exhibits are the **Seabird Aviary**, with rhinoceros auklets and tufted puffins, and mammal exhibits starring California **sea lions, seals** and **sea otters**.

Sea Lion Caves★★

About 40mi south of Newport. 91560 Hwy. 101 N., Florence. 541-547-3111. www.sealioncaves.com. Open year-round daily 9am–5pm. $12, $8 children (ages 3-12).

Just 11mi north of Florence, the largest sea cave in the country can be reached by an elevator that descends a 208ft cliff face to a viewing platform.

Inside, up to 1,000 boisterous **Steller sea lions** bellow loudly as they laze about on boulders and

Bandon Dunes Golf Resort

57744 Round Lake Dr., Bandon, off Hwy. 101. 541-347-4380. www.bandondunesgolf.com.

Ranked among the top **golf** resorts in the nation, Bandon Dunes is widely considered the country's most authentic nod to Scotland's ancient links. The setting, on a windswept, rugged coastline with grassy dunes rolling to the ocean, is spectacular; of the total, 12 holes meander along a 100ft bluff overlooking 23mi of ocean shores.

cliff sides. This sight is perhaps the coast's most iconic tourist experience.

Hatfield Marine Science Center★

2030 SE Marine Science Dr., Newport. 541-867-0226. www.hmsc.oregonstate.edu. Open late May–early Sept daily 10am–5pm. Rest of the year Thu–Mon 10am–4pm. $5 per person donation suggested.

At this headquarters for Oregon State University's marine-research program, some 200 marine scientists conduct research. The **visitor center** features hands-on exhibits on topics such as global warming. Of special attraction to children is the abundant marine life showcased in several aquariums.

CENTRAL AND EASTERN OREGON

Oregon divides dramatically along the Cascade crest. The western part of the state is a green land of farms, orchards and lush forest. East Oregon, on the other hand, is higher, drier land, more open and less populated, with vast remote reaches of desert nicknamed the "Oregon Outback." Oregon's central plateau was born of volcanic cataclysm and shaped by erosion, forces today evinced by huge cinder cones and still-visible lava fields. Bend is the region's hub and largest city. Farther east, Baker City is a historic waypoint along the Oregon Trail.

First settled after the Civil War, Central Oregon was sparsely populated for a century until a tourist economy took root in outdoor recreation in the 1960s. Long an Indian home, eastern Oregon was passed up by early pioneers en route to the fertile Willamette Valley. Later arrivals found this country excellent for ranching and mining.

Today, with 120 days of sunshine annually and plentiful outdoor recreation, including snow skiing, mountain biking, golf and white-water rafting, the **Bend** area is popular with outdoors enthusiasts, and retirees. To the southwest,

Mount Bachelor and the **Cascade Lakes** beckon anglers, skiers and hikers. To the south, the wildlife-rich Hart and Steens ranges thrust skyward. South of Bend, remnants of ancient volcanic activity can be seen at **Newberry National Volcanic Monument**. To the east, **John Day Fossil Beds National Monument** affords a glimpse into the distant past of this geologically rich area.

Despite Oregon's public image as a land of deep forests, almost two-thirds of the state lies within this vast, thinly populated, largely arid landscape of sagebrush and pine, hawk and coyote.

Floating the Deschutes River, Bend

©Pete Alport/Visit Bend/CCOP

Practical Information

When to Go

Late spring and early fall are the best times to visit, since the region is not as hot then, although Mount Bachelor draws visitors for the ski season. The average daily temperature in July in Bend is 82°F, yet 90°F and even 100°F days are common in summer.

Getting There and Around

♦ **By Air** – **Redmond Municipal Airport** (PDX) (541-548-0646; www.ci.redmond.or.us), 15mi north of Bend, is the region air hub.

♦ **By Bus** – Bend is served by the regional bus service **Central Oregon Breeze** (541-389-7469; www.cobreeze.com) from Portland.

♦ **By Car** – It's easiest to access the regions sights by private vehicle; car rentals are available at the Redmond airport (see By Air).

Visitor Information

Eastern Oregon Visitors Association (541-856-3356; www.visiteasternoregon.com).
Central Oregon Visitors Association (541-389-8799; www.visitcentraloregon.com).
Bend Oregon Visitor Bureau (541-382-8048; www.visitbend.com).

CITIES

BEND★

Visitor Center at 750 NW Lava Rd., at Oregon Ave. Suite 160. 541-382.8048 or 877-245-8484. www.visitbend.com.

Spread out within the eastern foothills of the Cascade Range, this high-desert community of 78,000 people straddles the banks of the **Deschutes River**, which cuts through the center of town. **Mount Bachelor** rises 22mi to the west, and the numerous attractions of **Newberry National Volcanic Monument** begin just 10mi south of town. Beloved by outdoor enthusiasts, the town serves as a base for skiing, rafting, hiking, bike-riding and other outdoor recreation. Bend is the epicenter of a region dotted with top-notch **golf courses**; there are more than 25 in Central Oregon.

The town offers nearly 50mi of urban trails, including the popular **Deschutes River Trail**. The town is also beloved by artists, who have galleries throughout town—many in the historic **Old Mill District**, a renovated retail and dining enclave sited along the river and offering splendid views of Mount Bachelor. On the opposite bank, the **Les Schwab Amphitheater** is the setting for outdoor summer concerts. Numerous parks snug up to the Deschutes throughout downtown, including **Riverfront Park**, with sand beaches and lush lawns. Bend is one of the few cities with a volcanic cinder cone inside city limits: **Pilot Butte** provides panoramic views of the Cascade peaks. For insight into the human history that created this burgeoning town, stop by the **Des Chutes Historical Museum** (*541-389-1813; www.deschuteshistory.org*).

BAKER CITY★

Visitor Center at 490 Campbell St. 541-523-5855 or 888-523-5855. www.visitbaker.com.

Shadowed by the Elkhorn Range of the **Blue Mountains**, this town sits at the eastern end of a broad prairie. **Oregon Trail** sojourners passed through here, but those who linger in Baker City today will find it an ideal staging point for exploration of the Blue Mountains as well as area history. The city boasts 100 heritage buildings, including the ornate **Geiser Grand Hotel★**, now restored. The official interpretive center (*see Historical Sites*) for the Oregon Trail lies 5mi to the northeast.

PENDLETON

Visitor Center at 501 South Main St. 541-276-7411 or 800-547-8911. pendletonchamber.com.

Pendleton is an Old West town that has never lost its historic past. It's known for its annual **Pendleton**

Oregon National Historic Trail

Pioneers seeking new land in the West once trod the historic Oregon Trail, which stretched 2,000mi from the Missouri River to Oregon; the first wagon train rolled along the trail in 1836. Today, remnants of the trail can still be seen in landscapes in six states. Bits and pieces of the Oregon portion of the National Historic Trail can be accessed by short hikes at a number of points in eastern Oregon. Go online to www. nps.gov to learn more.

Round-Up (*541-276-2553; www. pendletonroundup.com*), one of the largest rodeos in the nation. Real working cowboys, in Western wear, live in the region, and are a part of the daily goings-on around town. You're likely to run into them in **Hamley & Co.** (*541-27-1100; www.hamleyco.com*), a saddle shop where visitors can watch leather saddles being hand-carved. For thousands of years, Native Americans called this region home, and the superb **Tamastslikt Cultural Institute** offers a good introduction to their history. **Pendleton Woolen Mills** began crafting blankets for trade with Native Americans beginning in 1909 (*see below*). The **Heritage Station Museum** (*541-276-0012; www.heritagestationmuseum.org*) and **Pendleton Underground Tours★** (*541-276-0730; www. pendletonundergroundtours.org*), in the city's historic district, add opportunities to learn about town history and Western heritage.

Geiser Grand Hotel, Baker City

©Baker County Tourism – Basecampbaker.com

MUSEUMS

High Desert Museum★★

59800 S. Hwy. 97, 5mi south of Bend. 541-382-4754. www.high desertmuseum.org. Open May–Oct daily 9am–5pm. Rest of year 10am–4pm. $15, $12 winter.

This splendid, multi-faceted facility is both a museum and a wildlife park. Indoors, The **Hall of Exploration and Settlement** offers insights into the lives of those who lived in this High Desert region, through sights and sounds. Outside, **trails** lead to excellent animal displays in natural settings, including agile otters and birds of prey, and a historic **sawmill** and **ranch house** are settings for characters portraying turn-of-the-20C workers and homesteaders.

Museum at Warm Springs★★

2189 Hwy 26, Warm Springs. 541-553-3331. www.museumat warmsprings.org. Open May–Oct daily 9am–5pm. Rest of the year closed Sun–Mon. $7.

Designed to resemble a riverside encampment, this 25,000sq ft museum is a splendid architectural achievement from the outside,

and an achievement of a different sort on the inside. The museum contains one of the strongest collections of **American Indian** artifacts in the nation. Masks, ceremonial clothing and ritual implements are among the array of treasured artifacts on display.

Tamástslikt Cultural Institute★★

47106 Wildhorse Blvd., Pendleton. 541-966-9748. www.tamastslikt. org. Open Apr–Sept daily 9am–5pm. Rest of the year closed Sun. $8, free first Fri of the month.

Filled with artifacts, photographs and multi-media exhibits, the Tamástslikt museum illuminates the history of three tribes—the **Cayuse**, **Umatilla** and **Walla Walla**—who lived in the Pacific Northwest's Plateau region. The groups were in contact with the Lewis and Clark Expedition of 1804-1806, assisting the explorers on their journey. Some 40 years later the ruts of the Oregon Trail cut through their homeland. The 14,000sq ft museum is one of the best at recounting the Native American experience.

Courtesy of The Museum at Warm Springs

Museum at Warm Springs

HISTORICAL SITES

National Historic Oregon Trail Interpretive Center★★

22267 Oregon Hwy. 86, Baker City. 541-523-1843. www.blm.gov. Open mid-Apr–mid-Oct daily 9am–6pm. Rest of the year, hours vary. $8, $5 Nov–Mar.

Atop Flagstaff Hill, this interpretive center overlooks nearly seven miles of **Oregon Trail ruts** through sagebrush-dotted terrain. Multimedia exhibits, living history demonstrations and more than 4mi of interpretive **trails** explain the grueling challenges faced by pioneers traveling the Oregon Trail.

Kam Wah Chung & Co. State Heritage Site★

125 NW Canton St., John Day. 541-575-2800. www.oregonstate parks.org. Open May–Oct daily 9am–5pm.

In the late 19C, the Kam Wah Chung & Co. was a general store, doctor's office, and library that was the center of Chinese social and religious life for laborers who provided services during Oregon's gold strikes. Today a museum, the site is filled with more than 1,000 historic artifacts, many of them imports from China.

The two-story building and adjacent interpretive center illuminate the lives of proprietors Lung On and Doc Hay.

Pendleton Woolen Mills★

1307 SE Court Pl., Pendleton. 541-276-6911. www.pendleton-usa.com. Free guided tours year-round Mon–Fri 9am, 11am, 1:30pm and 3pm.

One of the few operating historic woolen mills still in existence in the US, Pendleton Woolen Mills, open since 1909, originally wove woolen blankets used for trading with Native Americans.
Today visitors can observe working machinery, and see historic Native American-inspired blankets at the mill's **Heritage Museum;** a seconds shop and retail store are also on-site.

Reenactors at National Historic Oregon Trail Interpretive Center

THE GREAT OUTDOORS

Newberry National Volcanic Monument★★

Deschutes National Forest, 1645 Hwy. 20 East, Bend. 541-383-5300. www.fs.usda.gov. $5/vehicle.

Ten miles south of Bend, volcanic activity has created a dramatic landscape. Here, entire hillsides are made of obsidian, **lava flows** stretching for miles are dotted by cinder cones, **lava tubes** are big enough to walk through, and forests are now lava casts. Located within Deschutes National Forest, the 55,500-acre monument encompasses the volcano's massive **caldera** and some of its flanks.

At the **Lava Lands Visitor Center★★** (*58201 South Hwy. 97, Bend; 541-593-2421; www.fs.usda. gov*), exhibits explain the volcanic forces and their impact on the landscape. The **Trail of Molten Lands★** interpretive nature path here winds through a lava field; an adjacent cinder cone, **Lava Butte**, is accessible by a road to the top. Within the volcano's caldera are two spectacular lakes, **Paulina**

Lake★★ and **East Lake★★**, both with campgrounds and scenic lakeside trails for hiking. The road to the top of **Paulina Peak★★** offers a **view★★** of the entire Newberry Volcano caldera, as well as hundreds of miles of high desert country in every direction.

One of the most impressive sights in the region is the 700-acre **Big Obsidian Flow★★**, formed 1,300 years ago; a 1mi interpretive trail crosses the shiny black landscape. With the aid of a lantern (*rentable for $5 from the check-in station*), visitors can take a self-guided walk through a mile-long lava tube, the **Lava River Cave★**. The cave's temperature is a constant 42°F year-round. Nearby, the **Lava Cast Forest** offers an interpretive loop trail that winds through a surreal landscape of crumbling lava where tree molds mark an ancient forest.

John Day Fossil Beds National Monument★

Three distinct units northeast of Bend; Thomas Condon Paleontology Center on Hwy. 19

Paulina Lake

between Dayville and Kimberly. 541-987-2333. www.nps.gov/joda. Monument open daily year-round in daylight hours; paleontology center open year-rounddaily 9am–5pm.

The **fossil fields** of this 10,000sq-mi national monument are among the most extensive in the world, notable for their complete sequences of plants and animals that existed during the "age of mammals," following the distinction of the dinosaurs. Fossils found here tell the story of the evolution of flora and fauna, as well as about the changing climate and ecosystems over a period of more than 40 million years. To date, fossils belonging to more than 2,200 species of plants and animals have been found at the fossil beds. The national monument encases three unique regions, all of which have **driving routes** and **hiking trails** to view the spectacular geological formations. The **Sheep Rock Unit** *(intersection of Hwys. 19 and 26)* offers the most extensive

introduction to the region; the **Thomas Condon Paleontology Center**★ *(open daily 9am-5pm)* here has murals, exhibits and a working lab filled with scientists making regular discoveries, as well as the historic **Cant Ranch House**. This unit also features dramatic cliff-top **views**★★ of the John Day Valley.

The **Painted Hills Unit**★ *(75mi east of Bend)* is famed for its spectacular landscape of rumpled hills splashed with vivid colors—gold, yellow, red and black; spring wildflowers in April and May add yet more vivid colors to the palette. The **Clarno Unit** *(Hwy. 218, 18mi west of Fossil)* is notable for picturesque cliffs; the .25mi **Trail of the Fossils**★★ is the only trail in the monument where fossils in the rocks can be seen.

Mount Bachelor★

Cascade Lakes Scenic Byway, 22 mi west of Bend. 541-382-2442 or 800-829-2442. www.mtbachelor. com. Day Ski Pass $76.

At 9,065ft, this volcanic cone has the highest-elevation **ski slopes**★★ in the Northwest. From November through May the mountain draws downhill and Nordic skiers, snowboarders and snowshoers. Its network of 10 lifts (including 7 express quads), provide access to more than 3,700 acres of terrain.

The resort has worked hard to attract freestyle skiers and snowboarders with a 400ft s**uper pipe** and a nearly mile-long terrain park. Skiing lessons are available. In summer, miles of hiking and mountain-bike **trails** offer high-altitude exploration.

Snowboarder, Mount Bachelor

©Mt. Bachelor/VisitBend/CCOP

DRIVING TOURS

Hart and Steens Mountains Drive★★

66mi Steens Byway; 49mi on Hart Mountain Rd. to refuge, then usually 25mi in refuge. Begin in Frenchglen, 183mi southeast of Bend, following US 26 to Burns, then south on OR 205. From there, both Steens and Hart Mountain routes are improved gravel roads.

Between the two mountains, in Frenchglen, the **Frenchglen Hotel★★**, a 1926 roadhouse still welcomes travelers to nightly ranch suppers and cozy rooms. A four-hour drive leads to two of the most remote—and most ecologically rich—preserves in America. At 9,733 ft and 50mi long, **Steens** is one of the largest fault-block up thrusts on the continent, riven by impressive glacier-carved gorges. A stunningly scenic **gravel road** reaches the summit amid 400,000-plus acres of federal preserve. The **view★★** from the top takes in the striking Alvord Desert 6,000ft below. At the western foot of the mountain, **Malheur National Wildlife Refuge★** harbors hundreds of birds, from pelicans to tanagers. **Hart Mountain Antelope Refuge★★** *(headquarters on Hart Mountain Rd.)* shelters 3,700 graceful pronghorn, as well as mule deer, badgers, jackrabbits, hawks, falcons and sage grouse in 278,000 acres of high desert.

⚜ Hells Canyon Scenic Byway★★

218mi. Take Interstate 84 north 2mi from Baker City to OR 86, the start of the byway. www.byways.org.

In the remote northeast corner of Oregon, the snow-capped, 10,000ft peaks of the Wallowa Mountains stand in stark contrast to the 8,000ft depths of **Hells Canyon★★**, America's deepest gorge. At the bottom, the **Snake River** cuts through ancient basalt layers. This drive offers dizzying views of the chasm from overlooks, and traverses a region with rock formations and signs of the **Nez Perce Indians** who lived in this dramatic landscape.

The route carves a semicircle around the Wallowa Mountains, from **Baker City** to **La Grande**, in the lush Grande Ronde Valley. Around the byway are **Hells Canyon National Recreation Area★★**, **Eagle Cap Wilderness area** and **Wallowa-Whitman National Forest**, all offering recreational opportunities.

Cascade Lakes Scenic Byway★

66mi. Take Century Dr. southwest out of Bend 4mi to the start of byway at intersection with Bachelor View Dr. www.byways.org.

Winding through the Cascades west of Bend, this 66mi historic highway features outstanding views; the road passes through a **volcanic landscape** dotted with 14 alpine lakes. On days when the waters are mirror-calm, many of the lakes reflect views of Mt. Bachelor, Broken Top and South Sister mountains. The surrounding pine forests are popular in summertime for their hiking trails and campgrounds, and the lakes attract boaters and fishermen.

SOUTHERN OREGON

Stretching 130mi along the California border, southern Oregon extends from Roseburg, Grants Pass and Ashland in the west to the Klamath Basin Wildlife Refuge and Crater Lake on the east side of the Cascades. In the east, alpine meadows and mountain lakes give way to the vast high desert of the Great Basin. In the west, the Umpqua and Rogue river valleys contain charming towns nestled in the rumpled rural landscape of the Siskiyou Mountains. River-rafting, winery touring, Ashland's theater arts and a concert festival in historic Jacksonville draw visitors year-round.

For more than 11,000 years, well before the creation of Crater Lake in its caldera, **Klamath and Modoc Indians** fought each other here. In 1869 they were forced to share a reservation before being banished four years later to Oklahoma. In the mid-19C, **gold seekers** from California headed north to Jacksonville's strike. Disappointed that the strike was short-lived, most prospectors returned south.

Those who stayed in the area found the valleys suitable for farms, orchards and vineyards, and the mountains rich in timber. Today what attracts visitors to this corner of Oregon is one of the country's finest Shakespeare festivals, staged in the town of Ashland. Jacksonville's allure is its gold-rush era buildings and a popular summer festival. Outdoor recreation is a magnet on its own.

Water-Power Flour

The water-powered **Butte Creek Mill and General Store** (541-826-3531; www.buttecreekmill.com), in Eagle Point, 12mi north of Medford en route to Crater Lake, offer a fascinating glimpse of yesteryear. Creaking belts, rotating gears and archaic mechanisms groan, whirr and rumble as they turn grain into flour at this rare working grist mill. The adjoining **antiques shop** is stocked with the mill's flour and local culinary goods, amid hurricane lanterns, tin plates and other vestiges of the past.

Butte Creek Mill and General Store

©Leslie Forsberg/Michelin

MUST SEE

Practical Information

When to Go

Crater Lake's **summer season** *(Jul–early Sept)*, when the roads are snow-free, is brief, with daytime highs around 67°F and nighttime temperatures at around 40°F. The weather is pleasant May–October in the rest of Southern Oregon, with temperatures in the 70s and 80s, and higher east of the Cascade crest.

Getting There and Around

♦ **By Air – Rogue Valley International-Medford Airport** (MFR) (541-772-8068; www.co.jackson.or.us) serves Southern Oregon destinations, including Crater Lake, 80mi away.

♦ **By Bus – Greyhound** (214-849-8966; www.greyhound.com) has regularly scheduled bus service among communities throughout Southern Oregon. **Rogue Valley Transportation District** (541-734-9292; www.rvtd.org) provides regional bus service to Rogue Valley communities, including Medford, Ashland and Jacksonville.

♦ **By Car** – It's easiest to access Southern Oregon destinations by private car; car rentals are available at the Medford airport.

Visitor Information

Southern Oregon Visitors Association (541-856-3356; www.southernoregon.org). For information about **Ashland**, call 541-488-5495 or visit www.ashlandchamber.com.

CITIES

ASHLAND★★

Located just 15mi north of the California border, this pretty town of 20,000 is tucked into a valley in the Siskiyou Mountains. The former trading post for flour and lumber has been slowly gentrified into a premier cultural center. Ashland's **Oregon Shakespeare Festival★★★** *(see sidebar)* is one of several thriving theater groups in the nation. The town is also home to many artisans, whose works can be found at 30 galleries in historic downtown, as well as at the **Schneider Museum of Art** *(1250 Siskiyou Blvd.; 541-552-6245; www.sou.edu/sma)* on the campus of **Southern Oregon University**. The museum's

500-piece collection focuses primarily on 20C works on paper. Downtown, boutiques, galleries and cafes cluster on both sides of bubbling **Ashland Creek**. The creek's water is naturally carbonated lithium water. A **fountain** on the town's triangular plaza spouts the famous water, and farther upstream the creek flows through **Lithia Park★**, a 93-acre preserve with a Japanese Garden, a rose garden, woods and picnic areas.

High above town, the **Mount Ashland Ski Area** *(541-482-2897; www.mtashland.com; day lift tickets from $36-$43)* is the only municipally owned ski facility in the West, with 200 acres of terrain, 40 open for night skiing. An 8mi paved road leads to the ski area.

Jacksonville

©Leslie Forsberg/Michelin

JACKSONVILLE★★

Five miles west of the business hub of Medford, the entire 1850s gold-rush town of Jacksonsville is a National Historic District. With more than 100 brick, 19C storefronts holding shops and cafes, the mining town retains a Wild West atmosphere. A **visitor center** at the old railway depot (Oregon and C Sts.) has walking-tour maps. **Trolley tours** *(May-Oct)* take visitors back to the Gold Rush days. The town is renowned as the home of the summer-long **Britt Festivals★★** *(541-779-0847; www.brittfest.org)*, featuring first-rate classical, blues, jazz and rock music at a pine-encircled hilltop under the stars. Patrons arrive early with blankets and picnic suppers to enjoy the warm evening air.

Four miles north of Medford, in the Central Point hamlet, the **Rogue Creamery** *(541-665-1155; www.roguecreamery.com)* produces award-winning cheese. Next door, **Lillie Belle Farms** *(541-664-2815; www.lilliebellefarms.com)* gives free samples of handmade European-style chocolates filled with fruit from their own farmland.

Shakespearean Ashland

After failing to turn its lithium-rich springs into a destination spa, Ashland followed the dreams of a drama professor and converted an old band shell into an outdoor amphitheater. There, in 1935, the city kicked off the first **Oregon Shakespeare Festival★★★** *(541-482-4331; www.osfashland.org)*. The regional repertory theater stages 11 plays in its three theaters *(Feb-early Nov)*; attending a performance at the outdoor **Elizabethan Stage** is a memorable experience. Four of the works performed annually are by Shakespeare; the rest, including contemporary works, are by other classic writers. On **backstage tours★★**, visitors learn about building sets, lighting, costuming and other behind-the-scenes tasks of theater-arts professionals.

THE GREAT OUTDOORS

Crater Lake National Park★★★

See National Parks chapter

Oregon Caves National Monument★★

77mi west of Medford off US 99. 541-592-2100. www.nps.gov/orca. Open late Mar–mid-May Fri–Mon 10am–4pm. Late May–early Sept daily 9am–6pm. Rest of the year hours vary. $8.50.

Deep in the Siskiyou Mountains, **marble caves**, bejeweled with stalactites and stalagmites, attract spelunkers and sightseers. On 90min **tours**, visitors climb 500 stairs, duck beneath low ceilinged tunnels and enter chambers like **Watson's Grotto** and the **Ghost Room**. Above ground, the park preserves stands of old-growth forest; the 3mi **Big Tree Trail★** leads to the widest-girth Douglas-fir in Oregon.

Rogue River★

Southern Oregon Visitors Assn., 541-856-3356. www.southern oregon.org.

This wild and scenic river, which flows from the Cascade Range to the Pacific, is one of the West's most popular rivers for ⚓ **rafting**. The muscular waterway cuts through wilderness frequented by deer, black bears and river otters. **Rafting trips** range from family-friendly half-day excursions to multi-day camping trips filled with bucking bronco-style rapids *(see website above for a list of rafting companies).*

Upper Klamath
National Wildlife Refuge

©Tupper Ansel Blake/US Fish and Wildlife Service

Upper Klamath National Wildlife Refuge

Headquarters in California, 20mi south of Klamath Falls via Hwy. 97 or Hwy. 39. 530-667-2231. www.fws.gov/klamathbasinrefuges.

The **Klamath Basin National Wildlife Complex**, spanning the border between Oregon and California, is a vast basin of shallow lakes and freshwater marshes that attract flocks of waterfowl in the fall—more than 6 million of them, including the American white pelican and several heron species. In the Oregon section, the **Upper Klamath National Wildlife Refuge**, canoeing is the best way to see wildlife. A marked 6mi **canoe trail** is open year-round; canoes can be rented from nearby concessionaires.

The Lower Klamath refuge was the first wildlife refuge for waterfowl in the country, established in 1908.

VANCOUVER★★★
AND VICTORIA★★★

Vancouver, Canada's largest Western metropolis (pop. 650,000), occupies a magnificent site along the Strait of Georgia, which divides the mainland from Vancouver Island. Founded in the 1860s as a timber-harvest site, the city is backed by the Coast Mountains to the north and the Cascade range to the southeast. Vancouver has assets other than its setting: a protected deep-sea port, easy access to the Pacific Rim, Europe and Asia, and a virtually snow-free climate. Anchoring the south end of Vancouver Island, Victoria (metro pop.360,000) faces the Strait of Juan de Fuca. British Columbia's historic capital is famous for its mild climate, beautiful gardens and British colonial traditions, which date to the city's founding in 1843 as a Hudson's Bay Company outpost.

Victoria centers on its **Inner Harbour**, where ships from around the world tie up, floatplanes ply the air, ferries dock, and flower baskets dot the cityscape. Many visitors do a **circle tour** of Vancouver, Seattle and Victoria; each city is one to three hours' travel time from the others. Originally founded by Canada's Scotch-English settlers, Vancouver has seen successive waves of immigration from East and West, all coverging on the grounds of First Nations tribes, mostly **Coast Salish**, who lived in the area for 9,000 years. The first European settlement here was not Vancouver, but Fort Langley (1827), a Hudson's Bay Company trading post 15mi southeast. Itself an HBC trading post (1843), Victoria considerable predates Vancouver, which did not exit until the early 1860s, when a sawmill was established at Burrard Inlet. *For wider coverage of Vancouver and Victoria and their many attractions, see **Michelin Must Sees Vancouver**.*

Victoria's Inner Harbour, with the Empress Hotel

©Leslie Forsberg/Michelin

Practical Information

When to Go
Spring through fall is an ideal time to visit; from mid-October to May expect rain, but little snow. July to Aug are reliably warm and dry, with average highs of 71°F.

Getting There and Around
• **By Air – Vancouver International Airport** (YVR) (604-207-7077; www.yvr.ca) lies 6mi south of downtown (30min away). Taxi fare to downtown averages $30-$40. Airport shuttles serve downtown Vancouver, as well as Whistler. On Vancouver Island, **Victoria International Airport** (YYJ) (250-953-7500; www.victoriaairport.com) is 15mi north of Victoria. Bus and shuttle services are available. **Kenmore Air Express** (425-486-1257; www.kenmoreair.com) offers daily 1hr floatplane transit between Seattle's Lake Union and Victoria's Inner Harbour.

• **By Ferry – BC Ferries** (250-386-3431; www.bcferries.com) has daily sailings between Vancouver and Swartz Bay; the BC Ferries terminal is at the north end of the Saanich Peninsula, 35min from Victoria on Hwy. 17. High-speed **Victoria Clipper** (Seattle to Victoria; 206-448-5000; www.clippervacations.com) and **Black Ball Transport** (Port Angeles, WA to Victoria; 360-457-4491 or 250-386-2202; www.cohoferry.com) serve the Washington and Victoria route. **Washington State Ferries** (206-464-6400; www.wsdot.wa.gov) has two sailings a week, with stops in the US San Juan Islands, between Anacortes, 80mi north of Seattle, and Sidney, BC, 30min north of Victoria on Hwy. 17. Reservations are advisable on all ferries, and essential May-Sept and holidays.

• **By Train – Amtrak** (800 872-7245; www.amtrak.com) connects Seattle to Vancouver, BC, with twice-daily trains.

• **By Light Rail – SkyTrain** (604-953-3333; www.translink.ca) is $9 for a **DayPass**, good for the length of its 28km route and return; one time fares are $2.50-$5. The fare includes **SeaBus** to the North Shore and Vancouver's bus system. The **Canada Line** transfers passengers between the Vancouver Airport and Waterfront Station, downtown; the ride takes 15-20min.

• **By Bus – Translink** (604-953 3333; www.translink.ca) buses, trolleys and shuttles connect to SkyTrain stations and tourist destinations in Metro Vancouver. On Vancouver Island, **BC Transit** (250-382-6161; www.transitbc.com) serves Greater Victoria, Sidney and Sooke.

• **By Car** – A car is convenient for Metro Vancouver sights, but not needed for Victoria. Car rentals are available at both of the region's airports.

Visitor Information
For BC, www.hellobc.com. For **Vancouver**, 604-682-2222; www.tourismvancouver.com; for **Victoria**, 250-953-2033; www.tourismvictoria.com.

NEIGHBORHOODS

Vancouver's **downtown** is a bustling workday district of office and condominium towers and high-style hotels bounded by Burrard Inlet, Stanley Park, False Creek and Granville Street. The centerpiece is **Canada Place★★** (*999 Canada Place*), a hotel-convention space mostly set on wharves; its huge white "sails" are an iconic image. Shops, restaurants and clubs occupy **Yaletown's** renovated warehouses. Hugging Burrard Inlet, **Gastown** dates to mid-Victorian times, and is home to the Water Street **Steam Clock**. A warren of Asian shops and restaurants, **Chinatown★**, is graced with the **Dr. Sun Yat-Sen Classical Chinese Garden★** (*578 Carrall St; 604-662-3207; vancouverchinesegarden.com*).

Kitsilano preserves early 20C Craftsman homes as well as the **Vancouver Maritime Museum★** (*1905 Ogden Ave.; 604-257-8300; vancouvermaritimemuseum.com*); the **Museum of Vancouver** (*1100 Chestnut St.; 604-736-4431; www.museumofvancouver.ca*), devoted to the city's history; and the ever-bustling **Granville Island★★** (*beneath Granville St. Bridge; 604-666-5784; public market open year-round daily 9am-7pm; www.granvilleisland.com*)

In **North and West Vancouver**, magnificent estates overlooking Burrard Inlet. Uphill is day-use ski area **Cypress Mountain★** (*6000 Cypress Bowl Rd.; 604-926-5612; cypressmountain.com*) and its splendid views of the metro area. Over on **Vancouver Island**, Victoria's **Government Street★** is the city's main shopping district,

Granville Island, public market

©Leslie Forsberg/Michelin

with tea and chocolate shops, as well as imported clothing. It's dominated by the stately **Empress Hotel★★** (*721 Government St.; see Hotels*), opened in 1908 as the West Coast flagship for the Canadian Pacific hotels chain; now part of the Fairmont chain, it remains famed for elegant lodgings and the daily **high tea** (*advance reservations required*). The 1898 **Parliament Buildings★** (*501 Belleville St.; 250-387-3046; www.leg.bc.ca; open late May–Labour Day daily 9am–5pm; rest of the year Mon–Fri 8:30am–5pm*). house the province's Legislative Assembly and government offices. Compact **Chinatown**, includes narrow Fan Tan Alley; Fort Street holds antiques and collectibles shops. South of the Inner Harbour, **Beacon Hill Park** has verdant lawns, decorative gardens and views of the Olympic Mountains across the Strait of Juan de Fuca.

PARKS AND GARDENS

⚘ Butchart Gardens★★★

800 Benvento Ave., Brentwood Bay, 13mi north of Victoria. Open year-round daily 9am; closing times vary. $30.20 mid-Jun–Sept, $16.70–$25 rest of the year. 250-652-4422. www.butchartgardens.com.

These internationally famous 50-acre gardens were started in 1904 by Jennie Butchart to beautify a quarry pit resulting from her husband's cement business. Today the family still operates the gardens, maintained by a small army of gardeners. The floral showpiece is the **sunken garden** with its extensive lawns, trees and exquisite flower borders. Other highlights are the **Rose Garden** with its rose-covered arbors; the secluded **Japanese Garden**, with bridges and a teahouse; and the formal **Italian Garden**, with statues and a lily pond. **Fireworks** are displayed in **summer** (*Sat night*), and at the holiday season, the gardens are festooned with millions of lights.

Stanley Park★★★

North of downtown Vancouver. Open year-round daily. 604-257-8400. www.vancouver.ca/parks.

This beloved park occupies 1,000 acres at the northwest end of the Vancouver peninsula. Trails crisscross the forested interior, and the **Stanley Park Seawall**★★ rims the shoreline. Horse-drawn **carriage tours** (*Mar-Oct; 1hr; $30*) depart from the Coal Harbour parking lot. Begin your visit at **Nature House** (*604-257-8544; www.stanleyparkecology.ca*), where exhibits describe the park's wildlife and ecology, and volunteers can answer questions about the park. Also in the park, the **Vancouver Aquarium**★★★ (*845 Avison Way; 604-659-3474; www.vanaqua.org; open Jul–Labour Day daily 9:30am–7pm; rest of the year daily 9:30am–5pm; $21*) focuses on Pacific and Arctic sea life. Daily shows, a 69,000-gallon tank, and the **Treasures of the BC Coast** gallery showcase beluga whales, sea lions and other marine life.

Courtesy of The Butchart Gardens

Sunken Garden, Butchart Gardens

PARKS AND GARDENS

MUSEUMS

Royal BC Museum★★★

675 Belleville St., Victoria. 250-356-7226. www.royalbc museum.bc.ca Open year-round daily 10am–5pm. $16 ($25.50 museum & IMAX).

This eminent institution, built in 1968, focuses on the natural and human history of the province. Exhibits devoted to **First Nations art and culture** include19C **totem poles** from all over the province, ceremonial **masks** and a reconstructed **big house** and pit house . On the second floor, a series of spectacular **dioramas** of the coastal forest and seashore regions includes animal, fish and bird life. The third floor is devoted to BC's human history. The **modern history galleries** depict BC's founding and growth through a re-creation of an early **19C street**, complete with shops, hotel, movie house and railway station. In the European section is a replica of part of George Vancouver's ship.

UBC Museum of Anthropology★★★

6393 NW Marine Dr., Vancouver. 604-822-5087. www.moa.ubc.ca. Open mid-May–early Oct daily 10am–5pm (til 9pm Tue). Rest of the year closed Mon. $16.75 ($9 Tue 5pm–9pm).

This seminal institution offers both a famous building—a striking post-modern 1976 design by native son Arthur Erickson—and a famous collection, perhaps the world's single greatest treasure of **Northwest Coast** indigenous art and artifacts. Reconfigured and expanded in 2009, the museum today affords visitors the chance to view towering totems, vivid masks, artful carved canoes and shaped boxes, and innumerable other gems of First Nations life. Bill Reid's astounding **Raven and the First Men**, a massive but evocative carved-cedar depiction of the Haida creation legend, is an evocative centerpiece.

EXCURSIONS

Pacific Rim NP Reserve★★★ and Gulf Islands NP★

See National Parks chapter.

Whistler★★★

78mi north of Vancouver by Hwy. 99; www.whistler.com.

This resort town, in a valley in the Coast Range, is one of the most popular **ski resort** in the world. With a pedestrian "alpine"

village at its base, fine hotels and restaurants, and two mountains to ski on, the resort draws travelers from around the world, especially Europe, Australia and the US. While the resort offers Nordic skiing, dogsledding, ice skating, and other activities, **Whistler** and **Blackcomb** mountains dominate the scene. Together, they offer 5,280ft of vertical rise; 8,171 acres for skiing; and 37 lifts, including the **Peak-to-Peak Gondola★★★** as well as 39ft of snow a year.

RESTAURANTS

Blending the rich bounty of its seafood, orchards, vineyards and diverse farms with a global cultural perspective, Pacific Northwest cuisine is among the most inventive in the world. From fast food to fine dining, its culinary ethos is fresh, flavorful and expansive.

Luxury	**$$$$**	**>$75**
Inexpensive	**$**	**<$25**
Expensive	**$$$**	**$50 to $75**
Moderate	**$$**	**$25 to $50**

Cuisine

Salmon, shellfish, berries and wild game were the mainstays of life for the Northwest's indigenous inhabitants, and this reliance on fresh, local ingredients infuses the region's dining menu today. The prevailing cuisine is called **Northwest Contemporary** *(shortened to Northwest in listings below)* in Washington and Oregon; the term **West Coast** covers a similar approach in British Columbia (BC). In both cases, chefs rely heavily on ingredients available fresh daily from local growers and providers: seafood, vegetables, fruit, even meats and poultry grown sustainably at local farms. Many chefs start their day with a visit to a farmers' market.

Fish and Seafood

Salmon remains the centerpiece of Northwest dining; although most salmon comes from Alaska or the upper BC coast, suppliers go to great lengths to ensure it is handled carefully and shipped speedily to restaurant kitchens. Most connoisseurs prefer king (chinook) or sockeye (red) salmon; other common types are silver (coho) and pink (humpy). Salmon is typically grilled over a gas or wood fire (the traditional presentation) or roasted, with simple seasonings. **Crab** is also ubiquitous—the main type is **Dungeness,** a sweet, meaty variety usually served steamed.

Other regional seafood delicacies include spot prawns, oysters, clams and scallops; as for fish, **lingcod**, true cod, black cod (sablefish), rockfish and halibut are delicious and distinctive. Lobster is not native to the North Pacific, so when lobster appears on the menu, it has been shipped 3,000mi from New England or Atlantic Canada.

Wines

Northwest **vineyards and wineries** (more than a thousand) are widely acknowledged as among the world's best, with pinot noir, merlot and pinot gris leading the way, as well as cool-climate varietals like sparkling wines, riesling and gewurztraminer.

Food Carts

Portland is a leader in the new phenomenon of gourmet **food carts**, found throughout the city offering everything from Southern soul food to South Asian provender. Food carts are multiplying in Seattle, Victoria and Vancouver, as well.

Reservations

In peak summer travel months and Thursday to Sunday any time of the year, reservations are essential at least a week in advance at top-notch, chef-driven restaurants. Monday to Wednesday offers a bit less demand, but reservations are advisable in summer and on holidays.

SEATTLE METRO

Luxury

Canlis
$$$$ **New American**
2576 Aurora Ave. N. 206-283-3313.
www.canlis.com. Dress code.
Much as famous personalities go by a first name only, Canlis stands alone among Seattle restaurants for its high-minded approach to dining. Emphasis is placed on procuring the best foods from around the nation, so the menu offers Nebraska beef and Maine lobster alongside Northwest salmon and oysters. Guests are requested to wear suits or sport coats, service is whisper-perfect, and the hilltop view—of Lake Union and the Cascade Range—is nothing short of jaw dropping.

Expensive

Dahlia Lounge
$$$ **New American**
2001 4th Ave. 206-682-4142.
www.tomdouglas.com.
Seattle's most iconic chef, Tom Douglas, whose name is synonymous with Northwest cuisine, hit a home run when he opened his flagship Dahlia Lounge, more than 20 years ago. The extensive menu ranges from Berkshire pork loin and troll-caught salmon to Douglas' famous (and city's best) crab cakes, alongside vegetables grown on the chef's farm. Don't leave without trying the famous coconut cream pie, made at Douglas' bakery next door.

Metropolitan Grill
$$$ **Steakhouse**
820 2nd Ave. 206-624-3287.
www.themetropolitangrill.com.
The best steakhouse in the city, the revered Metropolitan appropriately serves up beef from Washington State: custom-aged Double R Ranch beef, to be exact, mesquite-grilled over high heat, sealing in the flavor. Other classics abound, as well; the Caesar salad is tops. The interior resembles an East Coast chophouse, with gleaming brass.

Seastar Restaurant and Raw Bar
$$$ **Seafood**
2121 Terry Ave. 206-462-4364.
www.seastarrestaurant.com.
Neighboring the Pan-Pacific Hotel on South Lake Union, Seastar resembles an undersea garden with its glass decor and aqua accents. Sushi here is artfully fashioned from fresh-caught fish. Whether the dish is mahi mahi, spring Chinook or halibut, it's expertly prepared and presented with accompanying sauces—perhaps lemongrass-Thai chili or beurre blanc—that paint the palate with layers of flavor.

Canlis
©Danny Lund

Seastar Restaurant and Raw Bar

©Seastar Restaurant and Raw Bar

Tilth
$$$ Northwest
1411 N. 45th St. 206-633-0801.
www.tilthrestaurant.com.
Chef Maria Hines' ode to organic, sustainable foods sits inside a Craftsman-style home in the Wallingford neighborhood. Tilth was named in 2008 as one of the best new restaurants in the nation. Hines jumps tall buildings to offer high quality, making everything in-house, from jam and vinegar to cheese and even butter. Among the seasonal menu options might be local Skagit River pork shoulder, and in the fall, silky corn flan.

Moderate

Cafe Juanita
$$ Italian
9702 NE 120th Place, Kirkland.
www.cafejuanita.com.
Chef Holly Smith uses the best local, sustainably raised produce and artisan products from Italy to create bold, eclectic dishes. The rustic, lakeside setting is appealing, and the menu changes regularly. Among the standouts are rabbit braised in Arneis with chickpea gnocchi and saddle of lamb with gratin of turnip and quince-thyme mostarda. The fare is complemented by a lengthy wine list focusing on Northern Italian producers and Northwest varietals.

Cascina Spinasse
$$ Italian
1531 14th Ave. 206-251-7673.
www.spinasse.com.
Northern Italy's Piedmont region is the inspiration behind Spinasse, whose house-made artisan pasta places this restaurant firmly atop the pillar of Seattle restaurants serving exquisitely made, honest foods. Dishes—perhaps tagliatelle with braised pheasant and huckleberry or squash ravioli with sage—are accompanied by a short list of "secondi," from trout to steak. Considered a top date-night restaurant, Spinasse has a rustic ambiance, with antique wooden tables and chairs.

Flying Fish
$$ Seafood
300 Westlake Ave. 206-728-8595.
www.flyingfishrestaurant.com.
For about two decades, Chef Christine Keff has been bringing inspired seafood dishes with an Asian flair to the table, from wasabi-sauced albacore to Thai-style crab cake. The sleek, contemporary space of Flying Fish, in South Lake Union, has a trendy vibe, with chandeliers hanging from ductwork over tables filled with tech geeks and fans. Keff's adjacent retail store and takeout shop appeal to those on the go.

Terra Plata
$$ Northwest
1501 Melrose Ave. 206-325-1501.
www.terraplata.com.
Chef Tamara Murphy draws legions of fans for this romantic regional-

foods mecca in a triangular space at the end of the Melrose Market. Wood tables and rafters, an open kitchen and amber-colored pendant lights set the scene for dishes ranging from a water buffalo burger to a sophisticated smoky roast pig with chorizo and clams. Rooftop summer dining offers splendid downtown views.

Volterra
$$ **Italian**
5411 Ballard Ave. NW. 206-789-5100. www.volterrarestaurant.com.
This contemporary Italian restaurant, sitting in the heart of Ballard—the city's trendiest dining neighborhood—is a marriage of Tuscany's bold flavors with the largesse of the Northwest. Natural meats star in dishes such as wild boar tenderloin served with gorgonzola and mustard cream sauce; local berries adorn the Tuscan chestnut honey panna cotta. The setting, with crimson walls, is romantic; on summer days the leafy courtyard is inviting.

The Walrus and the Carpenter
$$ **Seafood**
4743 Ballard Ave. NW. 206-395-9227. www.thewalrusbar.com.
With whitewashed walls, the pared-down contemporary interior of this tiny slip of a restaurant belies the briny bursts of flavor found in diners' plates. This oyster bar's selection of Washington State bivalves amply illustrates how much variety there is in flavors. Other seafood as well as garden produce and local cheeses and jams show up as supporting members in the cast of small plates.

WESTERN WASHINGTON

Expensive

Allium
$$$ **Northwest**
310 E. Main St., Eastsound, Orcas Island. 360-376-4904. www.alliumonorcas.com.
Former French Laundry chef Lisa Nakamura has worked her magic in the San Juan Islands at her restaurant, which draws admirers from near and far. Great care is taken with the tiniest of details for dishes drawing from local farms and waters. Nakamura's clam chowder uses saffron grown in nearby Sequim, and clams from a Lopez Island family farm. The best seating is on the deck, overlooking vast stretches of water and islands.

Duck Soup Inn
$$$ **American**
50 Duck Soup Lane, Friday Harbor, San Juan Island. 360-378-4878. www.ducksoupinn.com.
Decked out in cedar wood near a duck pond, this country-style restaurant pleases locals and visitors alike with flavorful plates of rustic fare. The likes of lamb goulash and Lopez Island pork meatballs are served with housemade sourdough bread and a local-greens salad.

Restaurant Marche
$$$ **Northwest**
150 Madrone Lane, Bainbridge Island. 206-842-1633. www.restaurantmarche bainbridge.com.
Northwest chef Greg Atkinson opened this island bistro in 2012: it's evident it's a labor of love.

A remodeled old garage holds tables and chairs crafted from one Oregon walnut tree, and the color scheme was inspired by nearby Dungeness Spit. Locally procured foods are the order of the day, with dishes such as trout meunière and reef-netted salmon. Atkinson is sheer genius with vegetables: one bite of his delicate pea flan is proof.

Willows Inn
$$$ Northwest
2579 W. Shore Dr.,
Lummi Island. 360-758-2620.
www.willows-inn.com.
The San Juans became a culinary sensation with the arrival of Blaine Wetzel, former sous chef at Copenhagen's world-famous Noma. Wetzel forages daily for whatever is in season, plucking edible flower buds, overseeing the plantings in the Willows' garden and visiting island farms. The result? Dishes that rise to a new level—smoked salmon presented in a handcrafted wood box with smoke-wafting embers inside, and in fall, crabapples crushed so their juice heightens the flavor of the sauces. Sunset views are as gorgeous as the presentation.

Moderate

Ajax Cafe
$$ Northwest
21 N. Water St., Port Hadlock. 360-385-3450. www.ajaxcafe.com.
Tucked away near the waterfront at the base of a bluff, this bistro sits inside an 1880s building. Ajax offers hearty, rustic meals fashioned from what's in season nearby. Dishes include SpringRain Farm half chicken with roasted potatoes, or Northwest fishermen's stew. The setting is whimsical, with mismatched glasses and chairs, and silly hats for guests. With live music on weekends, Ajax is always a party scene.

Alder Wood Bistro
$$ Northwest
139 W. Alder St., Sequim. 360-683-4321. www.alderwoodbistro.com.
With its careful focus on regional foods, this petite bistro would be expected in a bigger city, but in this small town with farm roots, it's a fresh breath of air. Wood-roasted meats and salads using produce, cheese and nuts from local farms are at the heart of Alder Wood. You're just as likely to be sitting next to farmers as fellow foodies.

Jimella & Nanci's Market Café
$$ Seafood
21712 Pacific Way, Ocean Park. 360-665-4847. www.jimellaand nancis.com.
Equal parts seafood market and intimate corner cafe, Jimella & Nanci's, on the Long Beach Peninsula, is an unpretentious place with unexpectedly big flavors. In the seafood case, hand-lettered placards show the names of the fishermen whose catch is on display. That über-fresh seafood and other local provender go into a short list of dishes that includes a silken crab omelet and one of the best pan-fried oyster dinners anywhere.

Maxwell's Speakeasy + Lounge
$$ New American
454 St. Helens Ave., Tacoma. 253-683-4115. www.maxwells-tacoma.com.

Inside an historic eponymous building, Maxwell's evokes the roaring 20s, with chandeliers hanging from high ceilings to illuminate the dark wood-trimmed dining room. Hearty fare ranges from gourmet sandwiches to steak and seafood options, all expertly prepared with inspired touches, such as a chevre-cider sauce and smoked sea salt.

Sweet Laurette's
$$ French
1029 Lawrence St., Port Townsend. 360-385-4886. www.sweet laurette.com.
This 70-seat bistro is sweet in two ways: the ambiance is cheery, with tall windows and robin's egg-blue and saffron yellow walls, and the cafe, originally a patisserie, is known for its exquisite pastries. Meals of dishes such as braised Neah Bay halibut and mussels Dijonaise meld French influence with Northwest products.

The Four Swallows
$$ Northwest
481 Madison Ave. N., Bainbridge Island. 206-842-3397. www.fourswallows.com.
A half-hour ferry ride from Seattle, Bainbridge Island is home to one of the region's best restaurants. The 1889 William Grow House, with walls painted saffron yellow, makes a charming setting for this Italian-inspired high-end dining spot that offers locally harvested fish, oysters, mussels and more. Handmade lasagna and pizza add to the eclectic menu of Northwest specialties. In summer, sit outside on the wisteria-draped porch.

EASTERN WASHINGTON

Moderate

Milford's Fish House
$$ Seafood
719 N. Monroe St., Spokane. 509-326-7251. www.milfords fishhouse.com.
Brick walls and brass fixtures, as well as what seems like an entire forest of mahogany, give an early 20C feel to Milford's, the regional favorite for wide-ranging seafood from Maine, Brazil, Hawaii and other locales. The restaurant is famous for its thick-cut "shallow fry" calamari. Northwest beef and lamb round out the menu.

Whitehouse-Crawford Restaurant
$$ Northwest
55 W. Cherry St., Walla Walla. 509-525-2222. www.whitehouse crawford.com.
A historic, brick-walled mill and former furniture factory with soaring ceilings and massive beams is the dramatic setting for exceptional meals sourced from nearby farms accompanied by hyper-local wines. Situated in the center of Washington State's wine country, the restaurant has gained national attention for its focus on hearty seasonal foods, including a spice-roasted duck breast with huckleberry mostarda, and house-made desserts.

Wild Sage Bistro
$$ International
916 West 2nd Ave., Spokane. 509-456-7575. www.wildsagebistro.com.
Ensconced in an unpretentious, low-slung building, Wild Sage

dishes up some of the Spokane region's best bistro-style meals. The eclectic seasonal menu includes specialties such as the excellent Wild Sage burger, with Kobe beef and hand-cut fries, and coconut-curry pasta with prawns. Breads and desserts are baked in-house.

PORTLAND

Expensive

Andina
$$$ **Peruvian**
1314 NW Glisan St. 503-228-9535.
www.andinarestaurant.com.
An entrée of succulent lamb shanks, slow-cooked with cilantro-black beer sauce, is among the unusual dishes at this celebrated Peruvian restaurant. Cuisine here is a fusion of traditional South American-inspired dishes and Northwest ingredients. With linen tablecloths and simple wood furnishings facing a wall of windows, Andina has a refined atmosphere that completes the adventurous, worldly fare.

Clarklewis
$$$ **Northwest**
1001 SE Water Ave. 503-235-2294.
www.clarklewispdx.com.
A bustling open kitchen is the backdrop to this sleek, award-winning restaurant, which works hand in hand with local organic farms. Clarklewis spotlights the best seasonal fare, and prepares foods simply, with Italian and French nuances.
Whether the tagliatelle with braised lamb ragu or hearth-roasted pork shoulder with Bluebird Farms farro and sage sauce, meals here are memorable. .

Meriwether's Restaurant
$$$ **Northwest**
2601 Northwest Vaughn St. 503-228-1250. www.meriwethersnw.com.
Whether seated in one of three foliage-encircled gardens or in inside the historic Northwest Vaughn building, diners enjoy produce from the property's 5-acre Skyline Farm—inside Portland city limits—as well as house-made pasta, crab risotto and a short list of meats and poultry. For the restaurant's popular, occasional Sunday Supper series, the chef prepares artisanally procured foods using a wood-burning rotisserie and oven.

Paley's Place Bistro & Bar
$$$ **Northwest**
1204 NW 21st Ave. 503-243-2403.
www.puleysplace.net.
Chef-owner Vitaly Paley plies his trade inside a Victorian home in the Nob Hill district. The 50 seat restaurant has an aura of classic elegance that's reflected in the dishes. Diners begin with charcuterie plates—pâtés and terrines—and follow them with meats and responsibly harvested world seafood, such as seared tombo tuna with bacon, squid and Corona-bean stew. They can choose small plates or standard portions, making this high-concept restaurant quite affordable.

Moderate

Mother's Bistro & Bar
$$ **American**
212 SW Stark St., 503-464-1122.
www.mothersbistro.com.
While the dining room is immense, the ambience is cozy and intimate at this popular date-night

RESTAURANTS

Mother's Bistro & Bar

©Mother's Bistro & Bar

restaurant, where the dishes shine as much as the gilded mirrors and chandeliers. Home-style comfort food from the heartland reigns at Mother's, whether the table holds heaping plates of chicken and dumplings, Mom's meatloaf and gravy, or pot roast fashioned from braised short ribs.

WILLAMETTE VALLEY/ SOUTHERN OREGON

Expensive

Joel Palmer House
$$$ **Northwest**
600 Ferry St., Dayton. 503-864-2995. www.joelpalmerhouse.com.
Fourth-generation restaurateur Christopher Czarnecki comes from a family that's passionate about mushrooms. He carries on this legacy at the restaurant his father founded in a heritage home in Willamette wine country, pairing mushrooms with fine wines. The chef himself forages for the mushrooms and truffles that grace plates such as Joe's wild mushroom soup; scallop quenelles served with lobster mushrooms; and marinated sturgeon with sautéed mushroom duxelle.

The Painted Lady
$$$ **Northwest**
201 S. College St., Newberg. 503-538-3850. www.thepainted ladyrestaurant.com.
A sense of refinement is apparent from the crisp linens and swanky upholstered chairs of the dining room to the artfully arranged dishes at The Painted Lady, an Oregon wine country destination restaurant. The seasonal menu makes good use of local ingredients in preparations such as slow-roasted steelhead with wild mushrooms or butter-poached oysters with crispy leek. The overall effect is both delicious and romantic.

Inexpensive

Word of Mouth
$ **American**
140 17th St. NE, Salem. 503-930-4285. www.wordofsalem.com. Breakfast and lunch only.
Everything is made from scratch at this friendly neighborhood bistro that serves a wide range of breakfast and lunch items inside the narrow rooms of an old house. Breakfast brings the house special crème brûlée French toast, omelets and hashes; lunch features burgers, salads and sandwiches. Don't miss the hearty, house-signature clam chowder, served with toasted sourdough from a local bakery.

OREGON COAST

Moderate

Bridgewater Bistro
$$ **New American**
20 Basin St., Astoria. 503-325-6777.
www.bridgewaterbistro.com.

Housed in a red wooden building on a pier overlooking the Columbia River, this bistro ranks among Oregon's most scenic restaurants. Beneath soaring ceilings, diners can enjoy a diversity of regional foods in small plates such as Scandinavian pickled herring and Peninsula cranberry salad (with berries from nearby Long Beach Peninsula). Entrées include the house specialty: a spice-encrusted roast duck breast.

Local Ocean Seafood
$$ **Seafood**
213 SW Bay Blvd., Newport. 541-574-7959. www.localocean.net.
You can't get any fresher seafood than at Local Ocean, both a seafood market and cafe. Situated on the water in the charming Bayfront neighborhood beyond the Yaquina Bay Bridge, the restaurant has roll-up glass doors and vast windows that let in the sights of fishing boats bobbing in the harbor. Try a range of small plates—steamer clams, Totten Inlet mussels or pan-fried oysters—before the main course of seared king salmon, perhaps, or expertly grilled halibut.

Nehalem River Inn
$$ **Northwest**
34910 Rte. 53, Nehalem. 503-368-7708. www.nehalemriverinn.com.
In a tiny hamlet on Oregon's north coast, the Nehalem River Inn has always had a reputation for superb cuisine. It went one step farther in late 2012 with a dedication to grass-fed meats and local organic produce. The seasonal menu now features items such as roasted bone marrow with grain mustard, and Oregon sea bass with risotto,

roasted vegetables and beurre blanc. Linen tablecloths add an upscale touch, and windows offer views of coastal greenery.

Stephanie Inn Restaurant
$$ **New American**
2740 S. Pacific St., Cannon Beach. 503-436-2221. www.stephanie-inn.com.
With high-back upholstered chairs in crisp stripes, and Roman shades, the Stephanie Inn's restaurant has a European formality to it, yet the food is anything but fussy. The chef prepares a four-course prix fixe menu nightly, with a number of delicious alternatives. Among the mix might be a wild mushroom risotto, roasted tomato-basil soup, Dungeness crab cakes and chocolate decadence cake. The dining room is not on the ocean side, yet the cozy fireplace more than makes up for the lack of view.

CENTRAL/ EASTERN OREGON

Moderate

Amuse Restaurant
$$ **New American**
15 N. First St., Ashland. 541-488-9000. www.amuserestaurant.com.
Ashland has a reputation for its sophisticated theater offerings, and it has a restaurant to match that high standard. Amuse is a stylish, contemporary space with a changeable menu that includes dishes with a French twist. Order the duck leg confit with mustard spaetzle, or truffle-roasted game hen with fingerling potatoes and truffle butter. During summer ask for a coveted patio table.

RESTAURANTS

Gogi's
$$ **Northwest**
235 West Main Street, Jacksonville, 541-899-8699. www.gogis.net.
In a blue-painted Victorian house, Gogi's offers an intimate dining experience near the famed Britt Festival grounds. Produce from the chef brothers' one-acre Applegate Valley farm adds fresh, earthy flavors to inspired continental cuisine, from seared scallops with parsnips to grilled lamb loin with a red lentil puree. Be sure to sample the well composed and scrumptious housemade desserts.

Inexpensive

Deschutes Brewery
$ **American**
1044 NW Bond St. 541-382-9242. www.deschutesbrewery.com.
Bend is an outdoorsy place devoted to mountain-bikers and outdoors enthusiasts. Deschutes is the town's de facto gathering spot. Great effort goes into making foods in-house, including breads and sausages. Even the hamburger that goes into burgers is hyper-local, with cattle feed crafted from recycled brewery grains. The menu is what you'd expect—burgers, mac and cheese, fish and chips— but the execution and riverside ambiance are top-notch.

VANCOUVER

Expensive

Bishop's
$$$ **West Coast**
2183 W. 4th Ave. 604-738-2025. www.bishopsonline.com.
Impeccable service and an intimate atmosphere mark this high-end Vancouver institution. Owner John Bishop was one of the originators of West Coast cuisine, which, in Bishop's case, is based on organic regional ingredients. Artfully presented dishes on the weekly changing menu incorporate such local bounty as Salt Spring Island goat cheese, Dungeness crab, wild sockeye salmon and local chanterelles.

Blue Water Cafe + raw bar
$$$ **Seafood**
1095 Hamilton St. 604-688-8078. www.bluewatercafe.net.
This glamorous seafood shrine has been the centerpiece of Vancouver's gentrified Yaletown warehouse district since 2000. Warm woods and soft lighting enhance the cafe's wide selection. Its famed Blue Water Tower is a structure of chilled fresh fish, shellfish, sushi and Dungeness crab. Entrées focus on regional offerings: miso-crusted BC sablefish, Chinook salmon with artichokes in saffron consommé, Kobe-style beef short ribs, white sturgeon with braised cucumber and watercress.

Bishop's

©Jordi Sancho

C Restaurant
$$$ **Seafood**
1600 Howe St. 604-681-1164.
www.crestaurant.com.
Inside this striking industrial-chic dining space with floor-to-ceiling windows overlooking False Creek, chef Robert Clark's creative Northwest seafood takes on Asian accents. The restaurant's signature dish is seared scallops wrapped in octopus bacon. Lavender-cured halibut or albacore tartare might precede an entrée of seared salmon with summer squash tart and eggplant purée. Fruit-based desserts offer a light finish. Fortunately, there is a tasting menu if you can't make up your mind.

West
$$$ **West Coast**
2881 Granville St. 604-738-8938.
www.westrestaurant.com.
Deep flavors in simple preparations are the hallmark at West, which also focuses on local, naturally raised ingredients. Dishes include seared scallops with butternut squash purée, roast sturgeon in curry with pearl onions, and beef tenderloin with sautéed kale and chestnuts. The high-style dining room features red-tinged wood paneling, 20ft ceilings and frosted glass accents.

Moderate

Mill Marine Bistro
$$ **Pub Fare**
1199 W. Cordova St. 604-687-6455.
www.millbistro.ca.
Perched along the Coal Harbour promenade, this cafe serves time-honored pub food—fish and chips, ribs, pasta—with flair. The outdoor dining area, which looks across the marina to Stanley Park, is a delight during sunny weather.

Italian Kitchen
$$ **Italian**
1037 Alberni St. 604-687-2858.
www.glowbalgroup.com./
italiankitchen.
This sparkling, high-style bistro near Robson Street is packed every night with see-and-be-seen diners who enjoy both the glittering ambience and the savory food. Though the dishes are largely traditional, such as osso bucco, chicken saltimbocca and mushroom ravioli, the presentations are expert. Particularly inventive are the platters meant for sharing, which offer samples of four different pasta, meat or fish dishes. The gorgonzola polenta is memorably rich.

Vij's
$$ **Asian Fusion**
1480 W. 11th Ave. 604-736-6664.
www.vijs.ca. Dinner only.
Culinary zealots from across Canada line up outside this south-side shrine (Vij's takes no reservations) to sample chef Vikram Vij's inventive Pacific Coast take on Indian cuisine. All the preparations are based on familiar standards such as curries, but each is embellished by West Coast culinary ethos and Vij's fertile imagination. Beef short ribs, for instance, come in a cinnamon and red wine curry; lingcod is roasted with red pepper/saffron curry. Vij's opens at 5:30pm, but the line starts forming long before that.

VICTORIA

Moderate

Bon Rouge
$$ **French**
611 Courtney St. 250-220-8008.
www.bonrouge.ca.
French bistro food, highly flavored and wonderfully unfussy, is the mainstay at this brasserie near the Empress. The snazzy decor has lots of glistening metal and crimson accents, but the cuisine is down-to-earth. Try the sensational skillet-seared steak and frites, the cassoulet or the braised pork belly.

Camille's
$$ **West Coast**
45 Bastion Square. 250-381-3433.
www.camillesrestaurant.com.
Tucked into the garden level of a heritage building, this mainstay of Victoria's fine-dining scene is perhaps the city's most romantic restaurant. Its candlelit, eclectic decor provides a setting for savory regional cuisine that's equally enticing. To be swept off your feet, try the breast of duck served with bok choy, spaetzle and Asian pears or the rack of lamb with a fig and walnut tapenade.

Spinnaker's Gastro Brewpub
$$ **West Coast**
308 Catherine St. 250-386-2739.
www.spinnakers.com.
Housed in a Neo-Tudor building by the Inner Harbour, this brewpub features high-class pub fare and West Coast bistro cuisine such as pork tenderloin with yam fritters, or fresh seafood with herbs and local vegetables. The management is rigorous about seasonality, and has begun using locally grown grain

for baking. The setting provides a splendid view of the harbor.

Stage Wine Bar
$$ **West Coast**
1307 Gladstone Ave. 250-388-4222. www.stagewinebar.com.
Housed in a heritage building with lots of old-growth fir, exposed brick, mirrors and plank floors, Stage's name refers to the nearby Belfry Theatre. House-made charcuterie includes exotic Hungarian sausage; main entrées feature savory meats and seafood such as pork belly, octopus, scallops and tuna. The convivial atmosphere is always buzzing, but not overwhelmingly so.

Inexpensive

Red Fish Blue Fish
$ **Seafood**
1006 Wharf St. 250-298-6877.
www.redfish-bluefish.com.
Lunch only.
If this tiny bistro doesn't have the best fish and chips in British Columbia, it's close. Housed in a recycled cargo container on the docks near the seaplane base, the compact kitchen churns out stunningly fresh and flavorful fast-food seafood to steady lunchtime throngs of downtown workers and savvy visitors. All the seafood is sustainably harvested, and preparations have a mildly spicy flavor (wild salmon with smoked chile adobo). While the tempura-battered fish-and-chips is the signature dish, grilled fish and oysters, as well as savory chowders, are also popular. Seating is outdoors and lunch lines are long; best to arrive before noon or after 1pm.

HOTELS

From quaint B&B inns to big-city luxury hotels boasting world-class restaurants, Pacific Northwest accommodations are varied and inviting, appealing to travelers of all tastes and wallets. Whether overnighting in a rustic log cabin by a gurgling creek, or luxuriating in an opulent wine-country retreat, you're sure to find a gracious welcome—and no doubt local dishes to dine on and nearby outdoor adventure as well.

Prices and Amenities

The properties listed below were selected for their ambience, location and/or value for money. Prices (in US Dollars) reflect the average cost for a standard double room for two people (not including applicable city, state or provincial taxes). In all these places, June to September is **peak travel season**, and reservations are recommended well in advance. Many of these hotels offer special discount packages, so it's best to check online.

Luxury	$$$$$	> $350
Expensive	$$$$	$250-$350
Moderate	$$$	$175-$250
Inexpensive	$$	$100-$175
Budget	$	< $100

SEATTLE METRO

Luxury

Fairmont Olympic
$$$$$ 450 rooms
411 University St., Seattle.
206-621-1700 or 888-363-5022.
www.fairmont.com/seattle.
The city's premier luxury hotel sits at the heart of downtown. Its historic ornate Italianate building embraces refined rooms in neutral colors with thick drapes to hush outside noise. Amenities include a well-equipped health club and swimming pool. **The Georgian ($$$$)**, housed in a greenhouse conservatory-inspired space, features French cuisine.

Hotel 1000
$$$$$ 120 rooms
1000 First Ave., Seattle.
206-957-1000 or 877-315-1088.
www.hotel1000seattle.com.
Situated near the waterfront and Pike Place Market, Hotel 1000 is a sublime retreat with luxury touches such as cherry wood wardrobes and upscale bath tubs that fill from a ceiling spout. The **spa** offers more pampering. **Boka ($$$)** serves New American cuisine and craft cocktails.

Expensive

Inn at the Market
$$$$ 70 rooms
86 Pine St., Seattle. 206-443-3600 or 800-446-4484.
www.innatthemarket.com.
The Inn is a coveted boutique lodging at Pike Place Market that offers extraordinary views of the market, Elliott Bay and the Olympics Mountains. Rooms, in neutral tones, feature Hypnos beds and custom linens. Three on-site restaurants, include **Marché Bistro & Wine Bar ($$$;** Urban French) and **Café Campagne ($$$;** Classic French), both highly vaunted.

🛏 Woodmark Hotel
$$$$ **100 rooms**
1200 Carillon Point, Kirkland.
425-822-3700 or 800-822-3700.
www.thewoodmark.com.
Edging Lake Washington's shore,
the Woodmark assures that all
guests have views from their
rooms, which are furnished in
classic style in terra-cotta and
oatmeal colors. Service is key
at this luxury hotel; guests are
treated to late-night warm
appetizers and sandwiches.
Bin on the Lake ($$$) is
renowned for its wine list.

Moderate

Cedarbrook Lodge
$$$ **104 rooms**
18525 36th Ave. S., Seattle.
206-901-9268 or 877-515-2176.
www.cedarbrooklodge.com.
Amid 18 acres of lush landscape
near Sea-Tac airport, this lodge
emits a serene Northwest
ambiance. Floor-to-ceiling
windows, original art and public
"living rooms" with complimentary
snacks are a few of the perks.
Breakfast is included, and the
Copper Leaf ($$$) restaurant is
highly regarded regionally for its
farm-to-table cuisine.

Hotel Murano
$$$ **319 rooms**
1320 Broadway St., Tacoma.
253-238-8000 or 888-862-3255.
www.hotelmuranotacoma.com.
Complementing Tacoma's arts
focus, this design hotel has its
own eye-catching contemporary
art collection in the lobby. Rooms
come in tranquil earth tones with
orange and turquoise accents.
Bite restaurant **($$)**, with its own

glass art, is among Tacoma's top
restaurants, serving Northwest
specialties.

Inexpensive

MarQueen Hotel
$$ **58 rooms**
600 Queen Anne Ave. N.,
Seattle. 206-282-7407.
www.marqueen.com.
In a low-slung brick building
that was originally a parking
garage, the MarQueen features
large suites with original
hardwood floors, crown molding,
sitting parlors and well-stocked
kitchens. The decor tends toward
Old World, with subdued colors,
simple furnishings and antiques.
The property has a **spa** and cafe
on the premises.

WESTERN WASHINGTON

Luxury

Roche Harbor Resort
$$$$$ **44 rooms**
248 Reuben Memorial Dr.,
Roche Harbor, San Juan Island.
360-378-2155 or 800-451-8910.
This historic resort has one of
the most spectacular locations
in the state, with formal gardens
and a lively marina fronting an
island-dotted bay. A wide variety
of accommodations includes hotel
rooms, rustic cottages, condos
and modern village houses; all
are beautifully decorated with
contemporary flourishes.
Added benefits include a spa,
outdoor pool and **McMillin's
Dining Room ($$)**, serving foods
from local waters and fields

Expensive

Alderbrook
$$$$ **77 rooms &
16 cottages**
*7101 E State Hwy 106, Union.
360-898-2200. www.alderbrook
resort.com.*
Alderbrook lies two hours south
of Seattle, within a fir forest and
at the edge of the inland fjord of
Hood Canal. Rooms are done in
soothing sage with window seats
for views of the Olympics.
The **spa** and shore-side
pool provide relaxation. **The
Restaurant ($$$)** serves seafood
harvested from the canal or
Puget Sound.

Lake Quinault Lodge
$$$$ **92 rooms**
*345 South Shore Rd., Quinault.
360-288-2900 or 800-562-6672.
www.olympicnationalparks.com.*
This 1926 retreat, situated on
fir-rimmed Lake Quinault, makes
a tranquil getaway. Cozy, rustic
rooms are furnished with antiques.
Visitors can canoe or explore tall
trees along trails in the Olympic
National Park. For rainy days
there's a sauna and a games room.
The traditional specialty of the
Roosevelt Dining Room ($$) is
cedar-planked salmon.

Salish Lodge & Spa
$$$$ **84 rooms**
*6501 Railroad Avenue SE,
Snoqualmie. 425-888-2556 or 800-
272-5474. www.salishlodge.com.*
Overlooking Snoqualmie Falls, the
historic lodge exudes a timeless
Northwest ambiance. Luxuriously
appointed guest rooms have
fireplaces and two-person soaking
tubs. The full-service spa features

warm-water pools. **The Dining
Room ($$$)**, serves seasonal local
fare, including biscuits with honey
from the inn's own beehives.

The Willows Lodge
$$$$ **84 rooms**
*14580 NE 145th St., Woodinville.
425-424-3900 or 877-424-3930.
www.willowslodge.com.*
Surrounded by lawn and gardens,
the Willows sits in Woodinville
wine country. Rustic Douglas-fir
timbers and a massive fireplace
are accented by Native art in the
common spaces. Guest rooms are
sumptuous, with fireplaces and
garden views. **The Barking Frog
($$$)** bistro features local wines
and Northwest cuisine.

Moderate

Inn at Langley
$$$ **26 rooms**
*400 First St., Langley. 360-221-
3033. www.innatlangley.com.*
Floor-to-ceiling windows in guest
rooms overlook the placid waters
of Saratoga Passage, the decor
is Asian simplicity melded with
Northwest natural. The on-site
Restaurant ($$$), with a river-rock
fireplace, presents a seasonal local
fare like Penn Cove mussels.

Inn at Port Ludlow
$$$ **37 rooms**
*One Heron Rd., Port Ludlow.
360-437-7000 or 877-805-0868.
www.portludlowresort.com.*
Overlooking a calm bay on the east
coast of the Olympic Peninsula,
this Inn welcomes guests to
comfortable rooms with fir trim,
gas fireplaces, soaking tubs and
private balconies (for mountain
views). The inn is part of a complex

that includes a **marina** and **golf course**. The **Fireside** restaurant **($$$)** prepares organic local beef and lamb, as well as locally caught seafood.

Lake Crescent Lodge
$$$ 52 rooms
416 Lake Crescent Rd., Olympic National Park. 360-928-3211 or 888-723-7127. www.olympic nationalparks.com.
Built in 1916, the historic lodge is surrounded by forest on the shore of the eponymous lake. Guests can choose cottages, rooms in nearby 2-story houses or lodge rooms, which have a central bathroom. Adirondack chairs are positioned toward the lake. Notable for local foods, the **dining room ($$)** has an extensive list of Washington State wines.

Lakedale Resort at Three Lakes
$$$ 22 rooms
4313 Roche Harbor Rd., Friday Harbor, San Juan Island. 360-378-2350 or 800-617-2267. www.lakedale.com.
Lodging options at Lakedale include rooms in the log-walled lodge with its massive fireplace in the lobby; contemporary log cabins with attractive furnishings, and spacious canvas cabins. Surrounded by three small lakes in a mature fir forest, the resort also has a campground. Hearty breakfasts are complimentary.

Skamania Lodge
$$$ 254 rooms
1131 SW Skamania Lodge Way, Stevenson. 509-427-7700 or 800-221-7117. www.skamania.com.
This Cascadian-style lodge on a ledge overlooking the Columbia River is renowned for its river view. The **Waterleaf Spa and Fitness Center** and farm-to-fork cuisine in the **Cascade Dining Room ($$$)** add to its fame.
Rooms done in gold and taupe tones feature fireplaces and Pacific Northwest art. The 175-acre resort maintains an 18-hole **golf course** for guests.

Suncadia Resort
$$$ 254 rooms
3600 Suncadia Trail, Cle Elum. 509-649-6400 or 866-904-6301. www.suncadiaresort.com.
A 6,400-acre mountain luxury resort, the Suncadia overlooks the Cle Elum River from a forested hillside, in clear sight of the river valley and Cascade Mountains. Light-filled, contemporary rooms come with a soaking tub, outdoor balcony and gas fireplace; suites include a full kitchen with granite countertops. The resort **golf course** and fine-dining restaurant, **Portalis ($$$)**, offering seasonal fare, are added draws.

Inexpensive

The Bishop Victorian Hotel
$$ 16 rooms
714 Washington St., Port Townsend. 360-385-6122 or 800-824-4738. www.bishop victorian.com.
Each charming suite at this quaint brick inn bespeaks Victorian flair. With exposed-brick walls, period furnishings and fireplaces, the rooms feel cozy and comfortable. Mornings bring complimentary in-room continental breakfast delivery.

Shelburne Country Inn

$$ **14 rooms**

4415 Pacific Way, Seaview.
360-642-2442 or 800-466-1896.
www.theshelburneinn.com.
Built in 1986, the charming
inn is the oldest continually
operating hotel in the state.
Rooms, in muted colors of pink
and goldenrod, are accessed
via narrow hallways and creaky
stairs. Each room is individual,
furnished with antiques, period
art and claw-foot tubs. Guests
enjoy an extensive breakfast. The
**Shelburne Restaurant and Pub
($$)** specializes in regional cuisine
like Dungeness crab, mushrooms
and berries.

EASTERN
WASHINGTON

Expensive

🍴 **Cave B Inn & Spa**

$$$$ **55 rooms**

344 Silica Rd NW, Quincy.
509-785-2283 or 888-785-2283.
www.cavebinn.com.
Surrounded by vineyards on a
plateau high above the Columbia
River, this elegant inn is proud
of its views of the rugged
gorge. Architecturally striking
Cliffehouses have gold tones,
fireplaces and high ceilings.
Inn rooms, Cavern rooms and
yurts are other lodging options.
The winery, pool, spa and **Tendrils
Restaurant ($$$)** (think house-
made pasta and local beef)
are pluses.

Sleeping Lady

$$$$ **58 rooms**

7375 Icicle Rd., Leavenworth.
509-548-6344 or 800-574-2123.
www.sleepinglady.com.
Encircled by pines near Icicle
Creek, this mountain resort lies
minutes from superb hikes in the
Cascade Range. In winter, guests
Nordic ski from the resort. Simply
furnished rooms, in cool forest
colors and outfitted with down
comforters, are grouped in clusters.
Kingfisher Restaurant prepares
seasonal meals with produce is
from a chef's garden, open for
strolling. Rates include all meals.

Sun Mountain Lodge

$$$$ **96 rooms, 16 cabins**

604 Patterson Lake Rd., Winthrop.
509-996-2211 or 800-572-0493.
www.sunmountainlodge.com.
Perched high atop a mountain
overlooking Methow Valley, the
lodge shows off local artisan-
crafted functional pieces and art.
Built in national-park lodge style,
it has soaring, timbered ceilings
and massive windows. Western-
themed rooms come with sturdy
maple and cherry furnishings.
Lakeside cabins are popular with
families. The lodge is famed for its
winter Nordic ski trails.

Cave B Inn & Spa

©Leslie Forsberg/Michelin

HOTELS

Moderate

Freestone Inn
$$$ **17 rooms & 15 cabins**
31 Early Winters Dr., Mazama.
509-996-9306 or 800-639-3809.
Cozy cabins set in a pine forest
at this Western-style lodge offer
privacy and tranquility. Each unit
is equipped with a gas fireplace,
kitchen and contemporary
furnishings with rustic touches.
Lodge rooms feature lake views
and stone fireplaces. While there is
a pool, the lake attracts swimmers
on hot days. The **Freestone Dining
Room ($$)** serves hearty, French-
inspired meals.

PORTLAND

Expensive

The Heathman Hotel
$$$$ **150 rooms**
1001 SW Broadway at Salmon.
503-241-4100 or 800-551-0011.
www.portland.heathmanhotel.com.
Portland's leading luxury hotel, The
Heathman, built in 1927, boasts
elegant, Old-World ambiance.
The well-appointed guest rooms
feature dark wood furnishings
set against pale gold walls with
original Northwest art.
The hotel's spot-on motto is
"Where service is still an art." The
**Heathman Restaurant and Bar
($$$)** offers sophisticated classics,
such as bouillabaisse and grilled
Pekin duck.

🏨 The Nines
$$$$ **331 rooms**
525 SW Morrison. 877-229-9995 or
888-627-7208. www.thenines.com.
High atop the Meier & Frank
department store at the heart

of downtown, The Nines offers
contemporary luxury. Ivory floral
patterns on taupe wallpaper
backdrop elegant rooms with glass
chandeliers and contemporary art
by local artists. Sumptuous linens
and down comforters add a plush
factor to the rooms. In a multi-
story atrium, **Urban Farmer ($$$)**
specializes in grass-fed Oregon
beef and other local foods.

RiverPlace Hotel
$$$$ **84 rooms**
1510 SW Harbor Way. 503-228-
3233 or 888-869-3108.
www.riverplacehotel.com.
A Kimpton boutique hotel,
RiverPlace is situated alongside
the Willamette River. Guest rooms
are done in subtle, off-white hues,
with attractive cherry furniture; the
focal point is the gorgeous views
from floor-to-ceiling windows. The
hotel sits away from the busyness
of downtown, so while it's near the
city center, it feels like a getaway.
Three Degrees Restaurant ($$),
serves seasonal comfort foods
such as grilled Willamette Valley
leg of lamb. The eatery has indoor
and outdoor seating overlooking
the river.

Moderate

Hotel Modera
$$$ **174 rooms**
515 SW Clay St. 503-484-1084
or 877-484-1084. www.hotel
modera.com.
This swanky, contemporary
boutique hotel blends the best
of 1960s style with modern-day
comforts. The stylish, gray-tone
rooms have vivid orange accents
and faux fur throws, and the entire
hotel is filled with local modern

art—more than 500 pieces. Outdoors, fire pits attract guests returning from nearby performing arts locales. Indoors, the **Nel Centro ($$)** restaurant offers reasonably priced meals based on French and Italian culinary traditions, using locally sourced foods.

Inexpensive

Inn at Northrup Station
$$ 70 rooms
2025 NW Northrup St.
503-224-0543 or 800-224-1180.
www.northrupstation.com.
Vivid lime green, brilliant purple and other fanciful colors greet guests at this hip, all-suites boutique hotel in Portland's trendy Nob Hill neighborhood. The playfully decorated guest rooms include kitchens with maple cabinets and granite countertops, as well as contemporary art. Guests receive complimentary streetcar tickets; the closest stop is just outside the door.

WILLAMETTE VALLEY/ SOUTHERN OREGON

Luxury

Allison Inn & Spa
$$$$$ 85 rooms
2525 Allison Lane, Newberg.
503-554-2525 or 877-294-2525.
www.theallison.com.
This ultra-green Oregon wine-country resort is a luxurious contemporary lodging option for oenophiles on Willamette Valley excursions. The inn is among a few in the world awarded a Gold LEED certification for its adherence to eco standards. Guest rooms, in

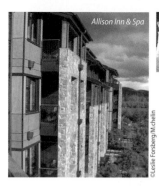
Allison Inn & Spa
©Leslie Forsberg/M.chelin

neutral tones with high-quality linens and original art, have window seats overlooking a hillside or vineyard. A **spa** and swimming pool add to the list of perks. **JORY ($$$)** blends wine-country cuisine with an 800-label wine list.

Moderate

Ashland Springs Hotel
$$$ 70 rooms
212 E. Main Street, Ashland.
541-488-1700 or 888-795-4545.
www.ashlandspringshotel.com.
Visitors to this 1925 hotel are forgiven if they believe they've taken a wrong turn and ended up at the estate of a wealthy naturalist. The lobby of this historic inn is filled with cases of butterflies, shells and other natural treasures, amid tall palm trees. Inn rooms, with saffron walls, sport botanical prints and muted, botanical-inspired bedspreads. Widely considered the best restaurant in the region, **Larks ($$$)** celebrates Oregon's farms, orchards and wineries.

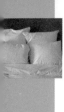

Country Willows Inn
$$$ **9 rooms**
1313 Clay Street, Ashland.
541-488-1590 or 800-945-5697.
www.countrywillowsinn.com.
Sitting at the edge of Ashland, this charming farmhouse offers an alternative to the bustle of downtown. Rooms, tastefully decorated in taupe, brown, beige and robin's-egg blue, are situated in a renovated barn, as well as inside the farmhouse; there's also a poolside cottage. The inn is known for its sumptuous breakfasts, which are included in the rate.

Inn at the 5th
$$$ **70 rooms**
205 E. 6th Ave., Eugene. 541-743-4099. www.innat5th.com.
This boutique inn is situated within Eugene's 5th Street Market, a warren of upscale shops and cafes. The spacious rooms, many with gas fireplaces, feature plush bedding and original art. Colors are neutral—beige and pale sage—with accent pieces such as red leather chairs. The cuisine at elegant **Marche ($$)** is French-based, with entrées such as wood-oven roasted salmon with chanterelles.

Inexpensive

Hotel Oregon
$$ **42 rooms**
310 NE Evans St., McMinnville.
503-472-8427 or 888-472-8427.
www.mcmenamins.com.
Occupying a four-story 1905 brick building that was once a bus depot, Hotel Oregon underwent an astonishing transformation. Today it is equal parts community gathering spot and historic wine-country hotel, with a **pub** on the main floor and cellar and rooftop **bars**. The **Paragon Room**, a billiards room during the daytime, becomes a live-music venue in the evening. The site's history lives on in vintage photographs and early 20C decor. Rooms are spacious, with chenille bedspreads and antique armoires. Some rooms do not have private bathrooms.

OREGON COAST

Expensive

Cannery Pier Hotel
$$$$ **46 rooms**
10 Basin St., Astoria. 503-325-4996 or 888-325-4996.
www.cannerypierhotel.com.
The sense of history is palpable at this contemporary luxury hotel built 600ft into the Columbia River, at the site of the old Union Fish Cannery. Historic photographs throughout lend atmosphere, as do the ships and barges constantly churning past. Rooms, in taupe colors, have viewing balconies. The town was once predominantly Finnish, and the complimentary continental breakfast includes Finnish delicacies; the **spa** features a Finnish sauna.

Tu Tu Tun Lodge
$$$$ **18 rooms**
96550 North Bank Rogue, Gold Beach. 541-247-6664 or 800-864-6357. www.tututun.com.
Decks outside guest rooms treat visitors to the roar of the Rogue River and the sight of deer grazing nearby. This timeless retreat is small enough for guests to meet all other lodgers at the nightly complimentary wine reception.

Lobby, Tu Tu Tun Lodge

©Leslie Forsberg/Michelin

If it seems that everyone already knows each other, it's true—couples annually book return stays at Tu Tu Tun. The lodge is known for luxurious, quiet rooms, some with outdoor soaking tubs. The onsite **restaurant ($$$)**, open May to October, serves local specialties such as grilled sturgeon and wild mushrooms.

Moderate

The Ocean Lodge
$$$ **45 rooms**
2864 Pacific St., Cannon Beach.
503-436-2241 or 888-777-4047.
www.theoceanlodge.com.
Situated on the oceanfront overlooking famed Haystack Rock, the lodge makes a calm getaway. A two-story rock fireplace and massive Douglas-fir beams dominate the lobby. Amenities include a library and always available freshly baked cookies. Guest rooms, awash in butter yellow tones with fir trim, have fireplaces and views of the ocean. Breakfast is complimentary.

Inexpensive

Overleaf Lodge & Spa
$$ **54 rooms**
280 Overleaf Lodge Lane, Yachats.
541-547-4880 or 800-338-0507.
www.overleaflodge.com.
Surf crashes over the rocky shore outside the windows of this oceanfront lodge. Comfortable, simply decorated rooms are done with ivory walls and bedspreads in warm hues. First-floor rooms have patios, allowing easy access to tide pools. The on-site spa's treatments include hydrotherapy. Breakfast is included.

EASTERN OREGON

Expensive

Pronghorn, an Auberge Resort
$$$$ **48 suites**
65600 Pronghorn Club Dr.,
Bend. 866-372-1003.
www.pronghornclub.com.
The stone-and-timber lodge buildings, with 1- to 4-bedroom suites, are tucked into the resort's lava and juniper high-desert landscape. All units have full kitchens and contemporary decor. The resort's two **golf courses** are among the most highly regarded in Eastern Oregon. Fine-dining option **Chanterelle ($$$)** boasts Cascade Mountain views.

Inexpensive

Old St. Francis School
$$ **23 rooms**
700 NW Bond St., Bend.
541-382-5174 or 877-661-4228.
www.mcmenamins.com.
Originally a Catholic schoolhouse, the property's 1936 building was

HOTELS

converted to a hotel. Guest rooms come complete with chalkboards in and student artwork on the walls. Extensively refurbished by the McMenamin lodging empire, the Old St. Francis today is a gathering place, with a **pub, brewery, bakery, movie theater** and immense **soaking pool** surrounded by tile murals.

Budget

Frenchglen Hotel
$ **8 rooms**
39184 Rte. 405, Frenchglen.
541-493-2825 or 800-551-6949.
www.oregonstateparks.org.
Closed Nov–early March.
This quaint wooden hotel in the Steens Mountains is a historic site operated by Oregon State Parks. The hotel offers simply furnished, rustic rooms. Dinner in the **dining area ($$)** is ranch-style, with hearty fare like roast beef, and homemade pies. Sign up in advance, since there are few dining options in this remote hamlet.

VANCOUVER

Luxury

Fairmont Pacific Rim
$$$$$ **377 rooms**
1038 Canada Place. 604-695-5300 or 877-900-5350. www.fairmont. com/pacific-rim-vancouver.
This sleek, high-style, high-tech hotel overlooks Coal Harbour and Stanley Park. Earth tones such as beige and sage dominate in the rooms, which feature an array of electronic amenities like remote control window shades and extensive audio-visual facilities.

Expensive

Fairmont Hotel Vancouver
$$$$ **557 rooms**
900 West Georgia St. 604-684-3131 or 866-540-4452. www.fairmont. com/hotel-vancouver.
The green-copper, turreted roofs of this downtown landmark have been an iconic city sight since Hotel Vancouver opened in 1939. Though the public spaces evince Art Deco stylings such as elaborately molded frescoes, room decor leans toward Edwardian elegance—burgundy satin bedspreads, floral patterns and walnut bedsteads. The hotel's cafe, **Griffins ($$$)**, is one of the best places for breakfast or lunch in downtown Vancouver, with a lavish, world-spanning buffet.

Moderate

Listel Hotel
$$$ **129 rooms**
1300 Robson St. 604-684-8461 or 800-663-5491. www.listel-vancouver.com.
With a location close to the West End and Stanley Park, yet within walking distance of the financial hub, this well-run six-story hotel attracts business travelers and tourists alike. Rooms on Museum Floors showcase Northwest Coast-inspired decor and art. Gallery Floor guest quarters feature original or limited-edition works from a nearby gallery. Artist Series suites each feature a different artist and design movement.

Opus Hotel
$$$ 97 rooms
322 Davie St. 604-642-6787 or 866-642-6787. www.vancouver. opushotel.com.
Deftly tucked into a historic Yaletown building, this hip lodging hews to a quirky ethos very popular with film, music and tech types. Room decor includes lots of polished metal and deep colors, including black, and the hotel provides an iPad in every room. The lobby, with a Gen X atmosphere, features settees and hundreds of votive candles. Service is personal and attentive.

Thistledown House
$$$ 5 rooms
3910 Capilano Rd., North Vancouver. 604-986-7173 or 888-633-7173. www.thistle-down.com.
Set amid lawns and gardens, the superbly renovated 1920 Craftsman-style mansion offers elegant, quiet rooms near Grouse Mountain and Capilano Canyon. Multicourse breakfasts feature such entrées as alder-smoked salmon omelettes and crepes primavera in chantilly sauce. Room rates include breakfast, tea and evening sherry.

Inexpensive

Sunset Inn
$$ 100 rooms
1111 Burnaby St. 604-688-2474 or 800-786-1997. www.sunset inn.com.
Its earlier identity as an apartment building means this economy hotel in the West End offers surprisingly spacious rooms, with simple furnishings in beige and walnut, and larger suites suitable

for extended stays. Many suites have kitchenettes; a laundry is an on-site amenity. Stanley Park lies just a few blocks away.

VICTORIA

Luxury

Sooke Harbour House
$$$$$ 28 rooms
1528 Whiffen Spit Rd., Sooke. 250-642-3421 or 800-889-9688. www.sookeharbourhouse.com.
This small inn and destination restaurant draw travelers from around the world. The owners pursue their vision of a menu based entirely on locally harvested ingredients. Organic gardens surrounding the inn supply much of the restaurant's foodstuffs. Deluxe rooms and suites overlook the namesake bay. The menu remains uncompromising in its innovative focus: nightly patrons of the **restaurant ($$$$)** are treated to octopus in aspic, sea cucumbers, grilled goat loin in scented geranium sauce, and other dishes.

Expensive

Brentwood Bay Resort & Spa
$$$$ 33 rooms
849 Verdier Ave., Brentwood Bay. 250-544-2079 or 888-544-2079. www.brentwoodbayresort.com.
Poised above a small cove in its namesake bay, this sophisticated lodge offers sumptuous accommodations near Butchart Gardens. Rooms and suites, all facing the water, feature fir-trimmed decor in earth tones. The **spa's** signature treatment is a hot rock massage with island basalt.

HOTELS

155

🛏 Fairmont Empress
$$$$ **477 rooms**
*721 Government St. 250-384-8111
or 866-540-4429. www.fairmont.
com/empress.*
Guest rooms in this landmark are
as elegant as the 1908 building
they occupy, with late Victorian
and Neo-classical furnishings of
walnut and brocade and a sitting
area. Resplendent with fine dining,
high tea (book well in advance)
and a **spa**, the grande dame is the
very definition of elegance. Higher
floor rooms are quieter, obviously.

Laurel Point Resort
$$$$ **220 rooms**
*680 Montreal St. 250-386-8721
or 800-663-7667. www.laurel
point.com.*
This glitzy, glass-and-steel complex
occupies a prime location at the
entrance to Inner Harbour, close
to downtown. Bright, spacious
rooms feature balconies and down
comforters. Exercise and leisure
facilities include a pool, saunas and
hot tubs. Outside, guests can relax
in the Japanese garden, graced
with a pond and waterfall.

Moderate

Fairholme Manor
$$$ **5 suites**
*638 Rockland Pl. 250-598-3240
or 877-511-3322. www.fairholme
manor.com.*
Built in 1885, the Italianate
mansion occupies a bucolic hilltop
in Victoria's Rockland district.
Annex apartments are done in
light woods, while the suites
have fireplaces, bay windows
and expansive baths; some have
decks and hot tubs. Breakfast is
complimentary.

Oswego Hotel
$$$ **81 rooms**
*500 Oswego St. 250-294-7500
or 877-767-9346. www.oswego
victoria.com.*
This stylish tower hotel, just a block
from the water, features snazzy,
fully-equipped suites in neutral
tones with kitchens, balconies
and exceptional outfitting—even
French presses for coffee lovers.
Though close to downtown sights,
hotel rooms are quiet.

Villa Marco Polo
$$$ **4 suites**
*1524 Shasta Pl. 250-370-
1524 or 800-663-7667.
www.villamarcopolo.com.*
Amid a gaggle of Victorian
and Edwardian inns, this 1923
mansion stands out for its
cheery Mediterranean character:
sunflower yellow stucco, tile roof,
airy common rooms. The four
suites are named after destinations
Marco Polo visited, and feature
appropriate decor; the Silk Road
suite, for instance, has hand-
painted murals of ancient world
scenes on the barrel vault ceiling.

Inexpensive

James Bay Inn
$$ **45 rooms**
*270 Government St. 250-384-
7151 or 800-836-2649.
www.jamesbayinn.com.*
This 1911 apartment-style lodging
complex offers affordable, quality
accommodation close to the
Inner Harbour. Rooms in the
main building are compact but
comfortable, and furnished in mid-
century style; the adjacent heritage
house offers more-deluxe suites.
Check for low off-season rates.

PACIFIC NORTHWEST

H

INDEX

List of Maps

Photo Credits (page Icons)

INDEX